Amy –
thanks for all
the help. Enjoy

David

Contents

Preface

I lived a rich and eventful childhood in the absence of money. Growing up in a small town of the Deep South after World War II was a bit like living in a turnip truck. I was happy and ignorant of most of what was going on in the world, and that wasn't all bad. I was but one turnip in a truck of 381 turnips, so everything in my world looked like, smelled like, and tasted like a turnip. It wasn't until I fell off the turnip truck in college that I realized there were other vegetables in the world.

My grandfather was a wonderful turnip. He was my best friend and primary caregiver while my parents worked during the day. He could neither read nor write, so he told me stories. Every day at naptime he would tell me powerful, scary, magical stories, and often fell asleep in our feather bed before I did. In the tradition of my grandfather's fanciful imagination I have mingled fact and fiction in this collection of short stories. His tales, which ignited my imagination and love for storytelling, are the inspiration for this book. 卐

Lucky Strike

"Cody is a good boy but he has a little streak."

I was so excited I could hardly sit at the Saturday morning breakfast table. I was nine years old, and had I been ten I think I would have known better than to execute the plan that was already beginning to unfold.

Our kitchen was small, the Frigidaire crowding the porcelain table and four red vinyl chairs. It was a warm and cozy room in winter but hot and stifling in summer. Air conditioning hadn't reached the tiny Texas town of Turnip.

This July 3 it was already warm at 8:30 in the morning. Beads of sweat were breaking out on my

1

face, and it wasn't just the heat. Tomorrow would be July 4, my father's forty-first birthday, and I had an early surprise for him. It was a surprise of such magnitude that my nine-year-old body quivered with excitement as my mind raced with laughter and fear.

Daddy was a big man and always sat to my left at the kitchen table, well within arm's reach. He laughed only when company came over, which was Christmas, Thanksgiving, and Mother's family reunion. Mother was seated across the table so she could fetch whatever any of us menfolk needed. She was a pretty woman with long, wavy black hair and a quick mind—a schoolteacher. She was always scheming behind my father's back, which kept him constantly in a bad mood. My brother, three years older than me, was seated on my right and in disbelief that I was foolish enough to play a joke on my father. After all, it was 1957 and a serious time for my parents. Their childhood had been spent in the Great Depression and their early adulthood in World War II, where Daddy survived the Battle of the Bulge but wouldn't talk about it.

Life was all fun and play for me. I had seen no pain. And today I possessed a cigar box full of fireworks and a plan.

We sat at our usual Saturday morning breakfast of biscuits, gravy, sausage, and eggs with almost no talking. Daddy didn't seem to like small talk— or large talk, for that matter. Daddy was a serious man, a man not to be trifled with, as everyone in town knew. He never showed affection to my mother and seemed only to be interested in scolding my brother Jim. But for the most part, he let me be me.

That was perhaps a mistake, for my grandfather said of me, "Cody is a good boy, but he has a little streak." Well, I felt the streak on this Saturday. Daddy was surly. And it was time to loosen things up.

Daddy was a smoker—three to four packs of Lucky Strikes a day, depending on his level of depression. Nothing "lucky" about them from my standpoint. The house billowed smoke like a Pittsburgh factory, and riding in the family Chevy was like sitting in the gas chamber. So the Lucky Strikes seemed the perfect target.

Daddy loved fireworks and associated the celebration with his birthday on the Fourth. Two days earlier I was buying fireworks when I noticed a new item of an explosive nature. It was a small, tobacco-colored "load" that could be inserted into the lighted end of a cigarette. I visualized tobacco confetti and was overcome with the idea. Then I realized the only smoker I knew and had access to was Daddy.

The nice thing about being nine is not thinking beyond the funny part.

I planned my event knowing that if I didn't see the explosion, it wouldn't be fun. But for it to be really funny, an audience would be required. I kept the secret, even from my brother, only to tell him just before we sat down at the breakfast table. I didn't understand Jim's fear.

So there we sat on a calm, warm Saturday morning at what might be my last breakfast. I had placed the Luckys between Daddy and me, with only one cigarette remaining so there would be no misfire. I knew when Daddy finished breakfast he would be left with his coffee and dessert cigarette.

I hardly knew what I ate. My brother was speechless and constantly glaring at me like I was an idiot.
Mother was trying to see that all was pleasant and
that nothing irritated Daddy. He seemed mad, which
was normal. No one ever knew what made him mad
or what would make him happy. I began to question
my plan.

As we closed in on our last bites, my anticipation
was growing with each mouthful I choked down.
Jim's eyes now showed total fear. Mother sensed
something, but I could tell she had no idea what was
coming.

Daddy laid down his fork and eased into his
chair. My body tensed. Mother picked up his plate
and headed for the sink. Daddy scanned the table
and looked at me quizzically as he reached for his
Luckys and Zippo, which I had arranged side by
side. He stuck the correct end in his mouth, just the
way I had studied his habit, and flicked open the
lighter with the familiar click that now sounded like
my death knell.

The little flame shot up. I couldn't breathe. As he
moved the flame toward his face and the bomb, my
stomach dropped. I knew I had made a grave mistake. I wanted to take it back, but it was too late.

I quickly glanced at Jim, who was ducking in horror under the table. Time was in slow motion. I
looked back at Daddy just as the flame struck the
end of the cigarette. Then, BOOOOM! The cigarette
exploded.

The big man jumped back in his chair. It was the
first time I had seen him frightened. Everyone had
jumped. The blast was ten times bigger than I

thought it would be. Tobacco was flying every-where—on me, on Mother, on the eggs, and all over Daddy. Bedlam was followed by absolute silence, with only the smell of gunpowder lingering. My ears were ringing. Everyone was in shock except for me, and that was where Daddy's eyes turned. My hand was over my mouth. Laughter would mean certain death.

I don't know what my expression was, but I suppose it was pure guilt. Daddy turned dark red, beginning at his large neck and continuing to the top of his balding head. He was speechless. Time had stopped. Death was imminent.

I thought of running. Too late. I thought of apologizing. Too early. I wondered how I would be killed, which seemed the next most likely event. But I was Daddy's favorite—would he actually kill his own son?

At that moment the unthinkable happened. He looked at me in what seemed to be a combination of disbelief and admiration. I thought I saw a faint smile begin to grow on his face. He lifted his big hand, and I instinctively moved back; then he bent down to dust his bald head. Unbelievably, he began to laugh. The man who never laughed was laughing. He needed to laugh.

I began to laugh, too. Mother and Jim were too frightened to laugh. Daddy and I laughed until tears of relief came from my eyes. I was alive. I had done the unthinkable to the unflappable and survived.

Then Daddy rose. I tensed. His laughter quieted and he said in a not-so-stern voice, "Cody, I suppose that was your idea." I looked at Jim, who had a look of "You had better tell the truth—fast." I dropped my head and said, "Yes, sir." Then he said, almost sympathetically, "Son, let's not try that again. Now, clean up this mess for your mother." With that, he left the room.

Jim almost fainted. Mother was slack-jawed, then said with the same intensity as if I had just run out in front of a car, "Andrew Cody, don't you ever do that again!" I felt as if the Death Angel had passed over without stopping.

For the next few weeks, each time Daddy lit a cigarette he checked both ends. I smiled inside only. I've never forgotten the moment when time stopped, and Daddy laughed. 🎴

Red's Jail

*"Well, Cody, Eunice built a jail out back from our house,
and every Friday she picks me up from work,
drives me home and locks me up 'til Monday."*

Red Burns was perhaps the kindest and most
generous man in Turnip. He also was the town
drunk. Red owned Turnip's Salvage and Dry Goods
Store, specializing in cheap. Red's store was located
on the poor side of the square, directly across from
Sam's Barbershop, and had a wilted front porch that
shielded the west sun and shaded the latest arrival
of bargains.

Red was a small man with a rosy face and a warm
smile. His head was bald, his eyes were usually
bloodshot but always twinkling, and he walked in
quick jerks like he was plugged into an electric
socket. He was mellow when sober and surly when
drunk. On more than one occasion I had seen his
wife Eunice drag him out of the store, place him in
the passenger seat of his pickup, then lock the
store and drive him home to sober up. Red had

had a running battle with the bottle that began when his six-year-old son Bobby, a year younger than me, was accidentally shot with his dad's hunting rifle.

Red's store was a two-aisle obstacle course of dented food cans, bent boxes, shoes that didn't pair, clothes that didn't match, toys that didn't work, and the occasional surprise of undamaged goods. Nothing had a price tag because Red liked to haggle. His joy was in sizing up the customer's wants with his willingness to pay. Red haggled down to the right price almost every time, often placing the merchandise back on the shelf several times during the negotiation. And if someone actually didn't have the ability to pay, Red would give them the item and whisper, "You go ahead and take this because I don't really need it. Just don't tell anyone I gave it to you." Red's lack of personal wealth never affected his generosity.

Every once in a while I went to Red's to investigate the latest arrivals, which he enjoyed discovering with me. But on many occasions the door would be locked. Through the glass front door I would see Red passed out in the middle of the aisle, surrounded by his treasures. I'd wait at the door long enough to see if he was breathing, then go about my other downtown adventures.

On a Friday night, Mother had dispatched my brother Jim and me to bed. The attic fan was pulling in the cool evening breeze through my window that faced the courthouse one block away. June bugs were bouncing off my screen, and lightning bugs were dancing to the sounds of locusts winding up and down in the pecan trees. I was waiting to hear from Red.

Every Friday night around 10:00, Red would chime in with nature's other critters and sing his mournful wail from the jailhouse window: *"Leeeeet meeeeee ooooout! Leeeeet meeeeee ooooout!"* Again and again Red's voice would rise and fall, modulated by his energy level as he begged through the bars. His mournful tone sounded like he was asking for his soul to be released from his body. Sometimes he would fall asleep first, and sometimes I would. I felt sorry for Red but, having visited the jail on several courthouse outings, I knew there was no way I could spring him from the heavy steel bars.

The Friday night ritual continued for years, and then it stopped. First, I wondered if Red's drinking days were over, only to see him later that week sprawled out on the store floor blowing bubbles in his vomit. Then I wondered if the sheriff had closed his office and jail which were located side by side in the courthouse. No, the lights stayed on twenty-four hours a day, and they were doing a steady business with one or two jailbirds a week peeking out the barred windows. I was puzzled.

My curiosity finally got the best of me. On Red's

next sober day, when he and I were rummaging through the new arrivals, I ventured, "I don't hear you anymore on Friday nights."

Red blinked a few times in confusion, then it registered, and he said sheepishly, "Well, Cody, Eunice built a jail out back from our house, and now every Friday she picks me up from work and drives me home and locks me up." He swallowed. "It probably sounds a little strange, doesn't it?" I nodded. "I've got a good bed, a bathroom, and a radio. She brings me home cooking . . . and a bottle. She doesn't want anyone to know." I blushed, but he turned even redder as we shared his embarrassment. He paused. "I'm drownin' in that bottle, Cody." Lowering his head, he began to weep softly. "I don't think I'll ever get over losing that boy." Tears fell with no words. Then he looked at me with red eyes, wiped his face, and pleaded, "You stay away from that bottle, Cody." He cleared his throat, regaining his composure. "And you be careful around guns."

"Yes, sir," I assured him.

For years after that I went to bed on Friday nights and thought of Red and his junk and his gentle manner and his mournful wail . . . and Bobby. Sometimes I still do. 🦴

Bull's Eye

"Can you believe the cojones on that son of a bitch?"

Ben and I were crossing the pasture with BB guns in hand, returning from an unsuccessful bird hunting expedition. As we walked in the knee-deep grass of the fenced pasture we kicked dirt clods, dried cow patties, or anything else of interest to make our trek less monotonous.

Ben stopped suddenly and put his hand on my arm, suggesting that I stop, too. His vision was frozen on a large Brahma bull about seventy-five feet from us, grazing head down with his butt turned toward us. He had the biggest sack of balls I had ever seen. Ben turned to me with eyes bulging through his Coke bottle glasses and excitedly whispered, "Can you believe the *cojones* on that son of a bitch?"

"Nope," I whispered out of the side of my mouth.

Then we turned, facing each other, and I could see we had the same idea.

Slowly we dropped to one knee in the grass and

11

quietly cocked our Daisy BB guns, contorting our mouths to try to quiet the mechanical noise. We were ready. I nodded and we took aim. Ben quietly counted with tight breath. "One . . . two . . . three . . . fire!" We pulled the triggers simultaneously, and then heard the double thud as both BBs struck the bull's balls.

The bull jumped wildly as we remained a one-kneed frozen audience, suddenly realizing we might have made a mistake. He kicked his hind legs then reared his front feet off the ground, twisting and jerking his head. He was definitely upset. With his butt still pointing in our direction he turned his head and spotted us. The glare in his eyes didn't look like a good sign. In one motion he angrily jumped to a position facing us that curiously looked like he was about to charge.

We held our breath. He snorted streams of snot and began slinging dirt one hoof at a time.

Our freeze thawed as Ben and I faced the fear in each other's eyes. Without a word we also jumped and turned in one motion and began to run. So did Mr. Bull.

As we ran for our lives, a thousand things crossed my mind. Why had I not stayed home and watched TV? Why had I thought shooting a bull in the balls was a good idea? Why had I not anticipated a chase and either shot from behind a fence or measured my speed and distance against that of a bull looking to get even?

It was too late. Ben was a step ahead of me as I spotted the fence. I was gripped with fear as I realized the fence might be too far away. My Keds were moving at top speed. I could feel the bull's weight jarring the ground and gaining on me. His heavy breathing grew louder and closer with each step.

Now in full panic, I visualized the bull's sharp horns and sensed his closure. The fence was nearing. Could I make it? Don't know. Could I jump it? Doubtful. No time to climb. No time to think. The bull was within spitting distance, but I wouldn't look back and risk losing speed or having a heart attack. Ben was now two steps in the lead as we both jettisoned our guns and hoped we could make the last few yards before being impaled. We were almost there—as was the bull. I could feel his hot, snorting breath on the backs of my arms. At almost the same instant, Ben and I dove under the lowest rung of the barbed wire fence, burying our faces in the dirt while sacrificing our shirts and stomachs.

Thank God we slid under the fence without getting hung up. The bull skidded to a hard and dusty stop, his huge nose about two feet from ours. He blew snot on our faces as he shook his horns at us. Our fear had only lessened slightly. The beast was enormous, and the glare in his eyes was terrifying.

We scurried to our feet and began running again in case the barbed wire fence didn't hold. When the distance seemed safe, we ducked behind a huge oak tree and eyed the bull. He hadn't moved and wasn't following, but he let us know his feelings as he continued his stare, threw more dirt, and shook his head daring us to return to his turf.

My back slid down the tree trunk as my legs began to fail. Ben followed. I raised a trembling hand to feel my pounding heart. Everything twinkled white. I wondered if it was the white light before death or if I had already died. My chest heaved as we sat speechless, leaning against the protective oak.

Simultaneously we peeked around opposite sides of the tree to check on the bull. He had given up, turned, and was swaggering away, swatting his huge balls with his tail. Ben turned to me, made a circle with his open mouth, and double-thumped his cheek. His re-enactment of the BBs thud released our tension, and we dissolved into uncontrollable laughter. Playfully shoving each other back and forth, snorting and twisting our heads, we embraced in laughter and rolled under the big oak tree, celebrating life. 🕸

Papa's Boy

"Life was simple and our needs were few."

The pace in Turnip was slow, as slow as the native ribbon cane syrup in winter, and changed only slightly with the seasons. My fifth summer was ending, and people in town moved slowly in the August heat. As many folks walked as drove, and I liked that.

The week before school started, Mother called me aside, which I thought was strange because she usually lectured Jim and me in pairs. The apologetic tone in her voice and eyes revealed the agonizing decision she had made to return to her school teaching career the following week. Jim was going into the second grade, and my losing him during the day would be bad enough. But with Mother leaving too, quiet desperation began to overwhelm me. She asked what I thought about her teaching, like she had done before Jim and I were born, but the tone in her question left no room for my opinion. So I simply asked who would take care of me. Her reply was "Mama and Papa, of course," her parents, my grandparents.

Mama and Papa had been integral parts of our lives but not for extended periods and not on a daily basis. My conversation with Mother ended with great reservations on both our parts.

My anxiety level rose as the first day of school approached. When it came, I was not ready. I was determined to do all within my power to see that Mother did not leave me. I sulked speechless during the one-mile drive to Mama and Papa's house as Mother strained to be cheerful in explaining what fun I would have during the day. I wasn't buying the spiel. I was not going to be at home; my dog and friends were not going to be close; Jim would be in school with all the kids, playing and having a good time; and Mother and Daddy would both be gone to work. It was more than I could bear. With my head drooped, tears began to roll down my cheeks.

By the time we pulled up to where Mama and Papa were waiting on their small front porch, Mother was in about as bad a shape as I was. My silent tears evolved into full-scale wailing as she walked away from the porch with Mama and Papa restraining me.

Mother knew she had to go. Mama and Papa knew they had to keep me. And I knew I had to stay. Even so, the next few days were difficult for everyone as I cried fervently each morning, begging with both hands for Mother not to leave.

Each day, when the little hand of the clock passed three and the big hand reached six, I knew Mother and Jim would drive up to take me home. At first I hated the slow, deliberate ticking of the clock.

It never once hurried. Then I began to adjust, and the hands of the clock moved faster. Before long I more than adjusted and began to enjoy my time with Mama and Papa so much I wanted the clock to slow down.

I soon became Papa's boy. He called me "Little Cody." He would say, "Little Cody is a good boy, but he has a streak!" He never defined "streak." Nor did he state it as a criticism.

The days began at 7:30 A.M. for Papa and me with a slow and easy breakfast. Homemade biscuits, homemade butter from Mama's churn, homemade jelly from the fruit trees, and ribbon cane syrup, which Mama would recook until it was so thick I had to cut it out of the jar with a knife. It was sweeter than store-bought candy. Mama and Papa stuck to the basics they had been raised on—eggs we gathered from under the warm hens; fresh buttermilk, which Papa liked best if it was still warm from the morning milking; and either bacon or a chunk of fried salt pork. Laughter and good feelings were always at the table. Even at an early age I could tell they were happy to have me in their house.

Most of my recollections of early childhood took place at my grandparents' house. Mama and Papa lived only a short walk from town—about a mile. Their house was situated on two acres which were put to their highest and best use: a small barn, a pasture for the milk cow, chickens fenced from the dogs, fruit trees, and one of the finest gardens in town.

Their tiny white farmhouse was a cozy place. Of its four rooms, none was larger than 10' x 10'. The house was warmed in winter to the point of suffocation by a gas space heater in the living room and a gas cookstove in the kitchen, which also warmed the dining room. The single bedroom, better known as the "north room," was closed off in the winter and only used at bedtime. I seldom spent a winter night there, but when I did, I distinctly recall the quick run on the icy floor to the bed and the layers of homemade quilts which were so heavy that turning in bed was almost impossible. It seemed strange to me that the room was frigid and yet I could blow smoke out my mouth. The room would have been unbearable had it not been for Mama wrapping the warm bricks she kept in front of the fire and placing them under the covers. Papa also helped by going to bed ten minutes before me and letting me have his warm spot so I wouldn't shiver.

In the summer the house was cooled by the breeze blowing through the windows that Mama kept propped up with small wooden sticks. A gentle breeze seemed always to stir on "Hooker's Hill," the local designation of Mama and Papa's farm. The ceilings were low and the floors were linoleum. Everything in the house was small but useful. There were no frills in the furnishings or decorations, and there were no frills in the bathroom, which was a small but clean two-holer located a short walk from the house, adjacent to the cow lot. Thank goodness one of the holes in the two-holer was small so I would not fall through. The small hole took care of my major concern; I had to live with my other outhouse concern—spiders. Winter was an especially thrilling time for a toilet experience. It was a miracle to me that a person could go at all!

Seasons were vivid at Mama and Papa's house. I hated baths at home until I had one at my grandparents'. Their bathtub was a galvanized No. 2 washtub. Water was drawn from the well and heated on the small cookstove. An adult could only bathe standing. The soap was homemade lye soap, and it felt something like sandpaper and acid. Baths were taken on the back porch. Modesty in bathing was replaced by my desire to survive. After a couple of wintertime No. 2 washtub experiences, I never complained again about having to take baths at home.

In the summertime we slept on their screened back porch because it was cooler. Mama had old iron beds with feather ticking that her mother had made from geese on their home place near Turnip. The beds were soft and fluffy and just right for Papa and me—and sometimes one of the dogs, if we could sneak it past Mama. Lying in the feather beds for afternoon naps and listening to the birds sing, the leaves clatter, and the nearby neighbors exchange pleasantries across the fences was calming. I felt safe at their house.

News only came our way by radio. They had no television. Only a few folks in town did. The local newspaper came once a week and contained no news of the world outside Hollis County. Mama and Papa's world was small, extending only to the county line. We didn't know much about robbery or rape or murder. We would hear some of that on the city radio, but we didn't know those people, so Papa directed our concern more to the weather and the grass and the garden. Life was simple. And our needs were few.

My grandparents had no car. Papa preferred to walk, and Mama had never driven anything other than a team of mules. Traveling for them amounted to a trip to Turnip once a week for groceries and occasionally to Evansville, thirty miles away, when a doctor was needed. Mother would drive them on those occasions. Restaurants, theaters, and telephones were not a part of their vocabulary. Toys were simple, requiring imagination and creativity: spools and string, sticks and a rope swing, and spoons to dig in the dirt. We built our own toys and cars and houses. We also had a little red wagon. Papa was the horse. He would tie a rope on the tongue of the wagon and would pull me over every inch of those two acres. With a blue second-hand tricycle and a few other toy trucks and cars, I wanted for nothing and had more than most.

Mondays were tougher than other days, especially if it rained. Papa called those "Blue Mondays." Neither of us liked them. They were only fit for dominoes, eating, and naps. The house was smaller on those days. But I always had a playmate. And I was glad he was sixty years older than me. He was gentle and patient and happy. I thought we were a good team. We made each other laugh, and we didn't need anything but each other.

Mama didn't have as much time to spend with me as Papa did. There was no retirement from cooking, cleaning, washing, gardening, and tending the animals. And she never questioned the custom. If

Mama didn't have a necessity in the house to attend to, she immediately got her apron, bonnet, and galoshes and headed outdoors. She loved to tend the cow and chickens and especially the garden. She and they fed us year round.

My grandfather was a small man, less than five feet tall. He was a walker as well as a talker. He walked with a bounce in his step and held his head high—not like a man of undue pride or authority but a man simply striving for altitude. He was bald on top where black, wavy hair once flourished, and varying shades of white hair rimmed his head. His face was round and appeared elongated as his chin graduated downward to his chest, which was smaller than his waist. His eyes were clear and clever, only obscured by delicate octagonal spectacles that left deep creases in the skin above his ears. He had no teeth, which caused his mouth to be slightly sunken, but that did not inhibit his intake of home cooking, as evidenced by a little round belly which bounced as he laughed.

Papa wore his pants high, higher in front than in back, with cuffs pointing up, well above the tops of his shoes. His pants were supported by suspenders—"galluses," he called them—that fit over a comfortable shirt or simply his long-handled underwear. His feet, hardly longer than mine, were well suited to his short, limber legs and his high step. He was a happy man and seemed always to have a tale to tell or a song to sing. His favorite songs were his own. Homemade and simple, like him. He sang them to Jim and me, and we loved hearing them, almost as much as he loved singing them.

Papa was a smart man but had no formal education. He never set foot in a school except to do the janitorial work and had no choice about it. His mother gave him to friends when he was five years old because old man Hawk, whom she had just married, didn't like Papa being around. The people he lived with were good to him but required that he work for his keep—picking cotton, chopping wood, and doing whatever chores needed doing around the farm. Papa was not bitter about his childhood, nor was he uneasy about his lack of education. He took pride in the fact that his five children never knew the hunger he had known, not even during the depression. He made a large sacrifice for his family when he sold their milk cow to enable his two oldest daughters to attend college. Mother, the younger of the two, began college at age sixteen, taught school part time at age seventeen, and graduated from college at age nineteen. Not long after graduation she purchased a house, not for herself but for Mama and Papa. They never moved from that house.

Papa's attitude toward work, which was instilled in his children, was "as long as you provide for your family there is no shame in hard work, no matter how simple." He enjoyed his work as janitor at the school and at the courthouse. He liked the people he worked around, and they liked him. He viewed it as having distanced himself from the nickel-a-day cotton fieldwork to an easy, good-paying job as janitor—no insignificant progression in his mind nor anyone else's who knew the cotton field.

Now retired and no less happy, he once again had

a job. Me. Taking care of his grandson. He had the time. And the patience.

Every afternoon my grandfather would take a nap with me on his screened back porch, just as Mother instructed each morning. Neither of us liked her telling us what to do—nor did we disobey. We would lie down on his feather bed and sink to the middle with ducking cloth walls on both sides. The little electric fan sitting on Papa's dresser, next to his cigar box filled with tobacco fixin's for him and candy for me, would purr a lulling song while Papa rubbed my back and told me "haint tales." He said they were true, and I feared that they were. "Bloody Bones and Skinny Eyes" was my all-time favorite. Papa was usually the first one to sleep, which was fine with me, but soon the rhythm of his deep, vibrating snore and the whirl of the fan made sleep irresistible.

My grandfather loved me, and I knew it. He would spend as much time with me as it took to see that I was entertained and happy. Games were our pastime and dominoes our favorite. He would play with me for hours, never complaining and with more patience than Job.

Another of our favorite pastimes was to take the dogs, Tinker and Bobby, across the road and into the Big Woods to hunt rabbits and "wompas cats." We didn't have a gun, but Papa would occasionally carry a butcher knife so I wouldn't worry too much about being eaten alive. We often saw some big holes that aroused the dogs and me, and Papa warned we would be in big trouble if that old wompas cat came out. I was relieved that he never showed himself.

As we walked through the woods, smelling

strongly of the sassafras trees, we would time our hunt so we could see the train go by. It was the Old Katy train, and the conductor was our friend although we had never met. We could hear him coming from a mile or two away, blowing his whistle. My heart began to pound when we felt the ground rumble as the train neared. The conductor would blow his whistle on seeing us, give a big wave, smile, and toss out a package of Juicy Fruit gum. Our eyes would follow him down the track until the red caboose was no more than a dot.

Papa would usually have to carry me home after our hunts for reasons of fatigue, which in fact was more fear of the wompas cat jumping out and eating us up. I felt safe on Papa's back, assured that the cat couldn't jump that high.

Moving trains, I loved. Stationary trains, I feared. Papa said I should stay away from parked trains. He said there were haints living in the boxcars, and he had the stories to prove it.

One of the most troubling events of my early life involved Papa and trains. During one of our hunts, after the train had passed, I secretly placed a penny on the center of the rail for the train to flatten on its next trip. I didn't tell Papa because I wasn't sure he would approve. After we returned home I began to worry about the train because I thought the penny might cause the train to turn over. The more I thought about the consequences, the more I worried until finally I began to cry. I begged Papa to take me back to the tracks, without telling him my reason, but twice in one day was too much. He said we would have to wait until tomorrow. I worried all night. The next day, as the train approached the penny, I grabbed Papa's leg—too scared to look. I held my eyes closed and was so relieved that no crashing sound came. Just the same old *clickety klack*. I was happy to see the caboose begin to disappear.

I rushed to the track to try to find the penny. And there it was, smushed into the size of a quarter and the thickness of a dime. I walked home that day with a pocketful of relief.

Somewhere along the way I lost that penny—that and my carefree childhood. I have spent the better part of my adult life trying to recapture the happiness and simplicity of those days, but it was not to be. They do live in my memory, however, as do Mama and Papa, the dogs, and a warm little house. 🦋

The Barbershop Mob

*"At the age of nine I had witnessed the
adult human as less than animal."*

John Downs is dead. He died in the state hospital
for the criminally insane. He ended up there because
one dark winter night he went home from work at
the barbershop, raped his mother, and knocked his
own teeth out with a hammer.

I was nine years old and John was twenty-two
when we came to know each other. He was not at all
violent then. But that began to change when he
started working at the barbershop.

Sam had the only barbershop in town, so every
breathing male as well as those who had drawn their
final breath were clipped by Sam. Sam offered three
haircuts, as the hand-painted sign on the faded green
wall clearly stated: regular, burr, and flattop. Only
the length of the crown was negotiable, with the
final decision left solely in Sam's hand and entirely
dependent on his disposition. Proper menfolk got a
haircut once a week, the tight-fisted waited two, but

only the poor waited longer than that. In Turnip, cleanliness was next to godliness, so a fresh haircut was somewhat of a religious experience.

Sam's Barbershop was located on the courthouse square two doors down from Turnip's only blinking light and 348 giant steps from my back door. I had deeply mixed feelings about the barbershop. It meant fun for me but was positively disdained by Mother. Men of low ambition kept long hours in Sam's, where cussing was as natural as snipped hair falling to the floor. Yarns spun there were intriguing as well as educational. Everyone knew the characters, at least when the story originated. The tales were noticeably tall, even to a boy my age, and the laughter of Sam's regulars at the crescendos in the stories made my insides feel good. But Sam's had a darker side, and it involved Sam's floor sweep and shine boy, John Downs.

John walked with a limp from a stiff right leg and held his right hand high against his chest with his little finger poking out to the side. He was an average-sized white man with big teeth, red acne, and a pudgy belly. His receding brown hair was combed from front to back, just like his boss, Sam the barber. John's eyes lit up like sparklers and his mind jumped from that of a child to an adult and back again. He wore brown high-top shoes that his mother had to lace for him and khaki pants held up by suspenders over his crisply ironed shirts. John's mother, a cook at the school cafeteria, made certain he was neat, clean, and presentable to the public.

My mother taught John in high school. He had tremendous difficulties with learning. She said John was never a discipline problem, even though he was continually picked on by other students. He had recently graduated from Turnip High School with an "F" average. The school didn't know what to do with John. Nor did the town.

Townsfolk considered John retarded and generally treated him with the courtesy they would a child. He laughed easily and often with a shrill giggle that sounded funny to me coming from a grown man.

John was limited in the places he could work. Mentally he wasn't suited for a white-collar job, and physically he wasn't capable of blue-collar work. He couldn't pass a driver's test, and even if he could, his family didn't own a car. Fortunately, he lived only a block from the courthouse square with his mother and sister. Their house was straight and sturdy, with even the front porch holding its own against time, but it looked as though paint had never touched the weathered siding. So John was, at least in the beginning, lucky to be able to work downtown in the barbershop.

John had a gift. His gift was more unusual than his ability to drink thirty-six bottles of RC Cola in a day and more unusual than drinking each one in a single gulp. John's gift was his memory, and his memory was unparalleled in town. John memorized every birthday in Turnip, all 381 of them, as well as the day of the week they occurred in any given year. When he correctly announced someone's birthday, it was customary to reward John with a nickel, which he immediately redeemed for an RC Cola at Dewey's Service Station. I envied John as he gleefully pocketed those nickels. That envy continued until the day I witnessed John's undoing.

My bare feet hopped from shade to shade on the scorching August sidewalk as I made my way to Sam's Barbershop, careful not to step on a crack, but more careful to avoid the fresh, brown tobacco juice in front of the downtown spit-and-whittle benches. As I pulled open Sam's screeching screen door, the old men seated inside muffled their laughter and turned their heads like owls on a roost to see who was coming. Sam froze from snipping Judge Forbes' hair and, with an anxious look, craned his head to see if Mother accompanied me. Mother was a church lady, and Sam had been well schooled by her regarding inappropriate language. To his relief and my delight, I was alone. Sam eased, realizing he wouldn't have to police either his language or that of his patrons.

Sam was a middle-aged barber with soft white skin and a gut that pooched beneath his priest-collared smock. He had strong hands, false teeth that rattled as he laughed, and sincerity that seemed doubtful, even to a boy of nine. His teeth clicked as he greeted me with an unusually chipper, "Hello, Cody. Have a seat." Gently closing the screen door, I stepped inside and sensed an unusual mood in the air, one I had never witnessed.

Sam's gang of regulars was there. The age and background of

the group varied dramatically, but their spirits were kindred. The voices in the barbershop were fanciful in the telling of tales, serious in speculation of sickness and death, and filled with hatred and supremacy when discussing other races. The mood today seemed a confusing combination of all those. It was to be my first encounter with a mob.

I walked past the gang of old men seated in Sam's Barbershop, uncomfortable with their scrutiny. My bare feet welcomed the coolness of the black and white checkered floor as the ceiling fan gently stirred the sweet smell of talcum and tonic about the room. I looked beyond the three white barber chairs to the mirrored back wall lined with multicolored bottles to see if Sam had my favorite purple hair tonic. I was in luck!

As I scanned the mirror, I saw John Downs busily organizing the rags, brushes, bottles, and cans at his shoeshine stand. He was the only one in the room who wasn't happy. I walked up to John, who was stooped at the powerful-smelling shine stand, and tapped him on the back. He jumped as if shot and turned defensively to protect himself. The gang snickered. John's fear vanished into a relieved smile as he recognized me. He swallowed and stuttered, "Heh-heh-heh-heh-woo, Mister Cody." I returned his smile and thought how odd it was for a twenty-two-year-old man to call me "Mister."

"Hello, John," I replied. His tension returned as his eyes darted around the room much like a steer in the butcher's holding pen. He cowed as he reached for his broom propped against the shoeshine stand and laboriously began to sweep, holding the heavy push broom in his good hand. Wanting to relieve John's anxiety, I offered my familiar, "John, do you know my birthday?"

He stopped sweeping. His mind escaped, and a full smile captured his face. Pulling his shoulders erect with pride and with eyes dancing like that of a child unwrapping a gift, John stated with confidence, "Oh-oh-oh-oh-oh yes, sur," trying to coordinate his memory with his mouth. "Yore birfday is Marg fof nineteen and foty eight. Wik dat means you wuz bon on a Chooseday, and in de year two fousand yore birfday will fall on a Sumday." He smiled a huge smile. I no longer verified the dates on the calendar. John was never wrong. I reached in my pocket and gave John the customary nickel reward. He inspected and pocketed the nickel, leaned his broom against the shoeshine stand, began limping toward the screen door, and made his customary announcement to the room, "Ju-ju-ju-jus wike Hank Snow's feme song, I gotta' be movin' on."

Sam briskly stopped him with, "John, you ain't goin' nowhere 'til you get this hair swept up!" John stopped and stood frozen in the middle of the room, reminding me again of the butcher's cattle when they reached the end of the chute and realized they were trapped. John hung his head, limped back to his broom, and began to sweep grudgingly. The gang perked up with Sam's control of John.

I didn't understand what was happening or why today should be different. John always immediately redeemed his nickel for an RC Cola, which only required a few minutes. I sat and watched.

John usually sang softly to himself while he

worked. Whether sweeping hair or shining shoes or cleaning the stained and bent brass spittoons filled with tobacco juice and cigarette butts, John was happy with his job and happy to be around the go-ings-on downtown. But not today.

Sam jacked the judge a notch higher in the chair and continued cutting hair in one clip, flicking three practice clips into the air above the judge's ear. The judge continually tugged at the full-length bib fastened tightly around his neck. Sam was laughing and talking with the gang. I could see the judge was concerned with Sam's lack of attention to his head, because the judge knew if Sam got carried away with his conversation a "regular" could become a "burr." Judge Forbes shifted in the chair to regain Sam's attention, but to little avail.

Sam and the five dawdling men in the shop began directing their attention to John, who, with broom in hand, was diligently trying to keep up with Sam's snipping and dusting of hair. Sam didn't like to walk on hair, as John was painfully aware.

Gib Franklin was the spark plug of the gang this scorching summer afternoon. Gib was a small man who walked like a banty rooster and talked like a cir-cus ringmaster. He had never worked for a living, only gambled and bootlegged. Gib climbed the shoeshine stand and sat like an emperor. John looked at Gib and said sheepishly, "Mister Gib, do you want a shine?" Gib slowly and deliberately shook his head side to side with a look about him that he wanted something else. Gib began flipping a nickel up in the air to get John's attention.

As Gib flipped the nickel upward with his thumb,

he asked, "John, would you like this nickel I got here?" John didn't reply, which I found curious because John lived for nickels and RCs. Gib raised his voice with a tone normally reserved for black residents of Turnip and said, "John, I'm talkin' to you, boy! Do you want this nickel?"

John stopped sweeping and gazed at Gib with a hollow look in his eyes, uncertain of how to react. John began to stammer and then said in a shy and humble tone, "Oh, yes sur, Mr. Gib, I shore would like dat nickel."

Gib smiled an evil smile.

"If you want this nickel, boy, then you're gonna have to sang me a song," Gib replied, eyeing his barbershop audience. John's face flushed and he began pushing his broom around the chairs in no pattern whatsoever, bouncing the bristles hard against the floor. Gib said again, "You hear me, boy? If you want this nickel, you gotta sang me a song!"

John looked up, much like a catfish seeing a worm on a hook and not knowing better than to resist. He hesitantly replied, "Whut song you wanna hear, Mr. Gib?"

Gib looked at the other men with a smile of accomplishment and gestured to the crowd, awaiting their request. Curly Pitts responded, flashing a broad whiskey grin, "We wanna hear a Hank Snow song, John, and we want you to sang us one real purdy-like," he said mockingly.

John hesitated, then wearily asked, "If I sang y'all one will you gimme dat nickel, Mr. Gib, ore you jus teasin' me agin?"

"John, you know I wouldn't tease you, boy. You

sang a Hank Snow song and this shiny nickel belongs to you. And you can go right on down and have you an ice-cold RC right now. You want an ice-cold RC, boy?"

"Oh, yes sur!" John said innocently, swallowing the hook into his belly.

"Then sang us a tune, and sang it good," Gib prodded.

John looked up at the pressed metal ceiling with the fan slowly clacking and began batting his eyes as he leafed through his Hank Snow repertoire.

"Come on, boy, we ain't got all day!" Gib blasted as his eyes surveyed the men who were now snickering and elbowing.

John's eyes remained focused on the ceiling as he began to sing. He sang from his heart the song he loved most—"I'm Movin' On." The crowd momentarily quieted. I was amazed at how well John sang, because his speech was so labored.

Then at Gib's encouragement, the mob began to hoot and howl. At first, John thought they liked the song.

Abruptly, Gib jumped down from the shoeshine throne, stopping John in mid-verse. "Boy, if you can't sang no better than that, you ain't gonna get this nickel unless you dance a jig, too! Yeah, you dance us a jig while you sang and I'll give you this nickel."

As the crowd jeered, John didn't know whether to laugh or cry or sing or dance. He stood there bewildered and helpless. Then Gib set the hook, "Boy, if you don't dance us a jig, I'm gonna have Sam fire your ass, then you won't *ever* have any more nickels."

I could tell John was close to tears as he began to dance for lack of any alternative. Every man in the house was laughing and clapping and pointing. Even the judge and Sam were joining in the gig.

I looked at every face and then at John. I knew what I was seeing was nothing less than the deliberate and calculated torment of a helpless soul who wanted only to be like everyone else. When I looked at John, I knew pity.

John was half singing, half crying, half laughing with the men, as he stumbled while trying to dance on one leg, a deformed arm held out to the side, with his push broom slapping the floor on the other side. My insides ached with humiliation for being part of the human race. I had never dealt with pity and rage simultaneously, so I simply sat and witnessed a scene that burned into my memory.

Before long Gib strode over to John, who had blundered to a stop, full of embarrassment and intimidation, unable to look at anything but the floor. The gang quieted. With his nickel rhythmically rising and falling in the air, then snatching it into his fist, Gib put his face directly into John's and said in a mean voice, "Boy, that was the worst sangin' and the worst dancin' I ever seen. There ain't no way I'm gonna give you this here nickel! Right, boys?"

"Right, Gib," came the replies. "That's right. Ain't no way he earned a nickel."

John became furious. His face turned beet red, but he didn't know where to direct his anger. I hoped he would shove his broom right down Gib's throat, but fear bested his anger.

John floundered, then pleaded, "But you promised me, Mr. Gib."

"I didn't promise you nothin', boy! Don't you dare tell me what I promised you!" he shouted, glancing at Sam.

At that Sam stopped laughing, pointed his scissors at John, and said, "John, don't you use that tone of voice on my customers or I'll fire your ass! You hear me, boy?"

"Yes sur, Mr. Sam," John paused, then unable to help himself, he pleaded, "but he promised."

Sam reached into his pocket, flipped a nickel on the floor, and said, "Okay, boy, there's your nickel. Now you get on outta here before I have to tell your mama you been causin' trouble."

That frightened and confused John even more. He hobbled over to the nickel and laboriously bent over to pick it up. Just as his hand reached down it, Gib kicked the nickel away in the direction of his audience who responded with a roar of laughter.

John followed the path of the nickel, never looking up. It was obvious he had been here before and knew the sooner he got the nickel the sooner he could get out the door.

The hockey game continued. It was hobble, bend, reach, then kick. Hobble, bend, kick. Faster hobble, bend, kick. Stumble, bend, kick. John finally had enough. He was furious. White foam was coming out both corners of his mouth. He stood up, his look piercing the faces of the men. He appeared deadly violent to me.

The mob realized they had pushed him too far. They backed off as he stooped one last time and grabbed the nickel from the floor. As he hobbled quickly toward the door, the mob spat their last barbs as Gib followed one step behind John, mimicking his walk and arm movement. John was purple with rage and mumbling as the door slammed behind him.

Then the laughing and backslapping broke out.

I bowed my head. My heart hurt. At the age of nine I had witnessed the adult human as less than animal. I was sad, disgusted, and sick to the point of vomiting. These were full-grown men, some of whom I had admired. I wondered how they could do what they had done—and enjoy it.

I observed evil that day. Before then I had thought it was bad being retarded. I was wrong.

I met John on the street the next day as he headed to work at Sam's. I was surprised to see the same innocent look in his eyes that he always had. He greeted me in his customary manner, "Heh-heh-heh-heh-woo, Mr. Cody."

I smiled. John had not visibly changed, thank God. But I had. ✺

The Secret of the Ice House

"Stolen always tastes sweeter."

Hollis County was a God-fearing community that allowed no beer, wine, or whiskey to be sold or consumed within its borders. Turnip was the county seat and boasted the county's only jail for those who transgressed that or any other laws.

Daddy didn't drink but probably should have in order to tolerate Mother's ways. Mother was a schoolteacher and church lady, so she couldn't have any fun. My brother Jim was twelve, three years older than me, and our concern with alcohol was to be sure we had an ample supply of empties for target practice with our BB guns. So, the selling and drinking of alcohol had held no interest to me until one scorching summer afternoon.

I sat on the loading dock of the Turnip Depot waiting to snoop around the Old Katy train as she made her two o'clock stop, sometime between three and dark. With no breeze blowing and only the smell of creosote bubbling out of the railroad ties below my dangling feet, I pondered the ice house across the tracks.

I was well within hollering distance of Tug Malone and Hack McBee as they sat propped back in the shade of the tiny ice house porch. Hack and Tug seemed unusually happy and prosperous for a couple of bulging middle-aged guys who operated the only ice house in the county and managed to work only a few hours a day. I decided my mission for this lazy Wednesday in July was to figure out the ice house business, because something just didn't add up.

I had been to the ice house many times. Mother and Daddy did not want me to go there, but they never said why. I had little interest in going anyway because there was no Coke machine, no candy case, and no bathroom. The place consisted of a flimsy wooden front porch, an office barely big enough for the cash register, and the ice-cold chiller room that was darker than death if the single naked light bulb was not turned on.

As I sat watching Hack and Tug, it occurred to me they were pretty content, particularly considering that no customers were buying ice, the only commodity they sold other than watermelons from the local melon patches. This time of year the little ice house was stacked high with blocks of ice on one side and dark green Black Diamond watermelons on the other. The porch was also lined with a few prize melons, the only advertisement necessary in Turnip.

Hot melons were one cent a pound, and cold ones were two.

That seemed cheap enough unless field theft was an option, which was always my best friend Ben's first choice. Stolen did seem to taste a little sweeter, and theft was simple. We'd park our bikes in the bushes, scan the field for the farmer, and slip through the barbed wire. Then we'd run across the blazing sugar sand until we located the biggest one we could carry, pull it off the vine, and carry the slick-skinned, gritty prize to the nearest shade tree, where we'd drop it from about waist high and run our bare hands in to pull out the seedless heart of the melon and shove as much as possible into our mouths. Juice all over our grinning faces was not a matter of concern. We were free, we were eating free, and we had outfoxed the farmer. It seemed a wonderful combination of accomplishments.

Hack was now dozing, and Tug was filling the air with his Lucky Strikes. Old man Daugherty drove up in his green pickup, but Hack never budged. Tug flicked his cigarette onto the dirt road in front of the pickup and spoke for a moment to Mr. Daugherty, nodded, then reached for the ice tongs on the wall and disappeared into the cooler.

The door had hardly closed when Tug reappeared with a heavy block of ice hanging from the tongs. He set it down on the wooden porch, pulled his ice pick from the place he always stuck it in the wall, and with a few deft stabs split the chunk down the middle. He then fetched a brown bag from the office and ran his arm inside to fluff the sack. He placed the bag under the grinder and pulled the sparking switch to start the pulleys. He tonged one of the ice halves and with both hands lifted it to about head height, placing it into the galvanized bin. The grinding commenced, and the bag below began to fatten. As the ice made its way down the grinder chute, Tug lifted and released the bag several times to assure a proper fill with no tipping over. As the first ice chunk disappeared, Tug lifted the other chunk into the hopper and repeated his sack-jostling routine. When no sound came from the grinder, Tug flipped the switch off and slid the bag from beneath the galvanized chute, banged it on the floor a couple more times, and rolled the top of the sack closed.

Mr. Daugherty handed Tug what must have been a quarter because no change was returned, and in the history of Turnip no tip had ever been given. They exchanged words and shook hands. Tug chuckled and loaded the bag of ice into the cab of the truck. With a friendly wave from Tug and a tip of the hat from Mr. Daugherty, the truck slowly moved down the dirt road, hardly stirring any dust. Tug lit another cigarette and propped himself against the wall on the back legs of his chair, resting his head against the whitewashed wood siding.

As I thought about it, Tug and Hack had the only partnership in town, and yet Tug did all the work. Hack had the only car of the twosome and kept it parked mostly hidden to the side of the store. They didn't work many hours and some days not at all. When they did work, it was more nap than work. They seemed to require more sleep than most men their age, and they also appeared unusually serious at times for no apparent reason. From all I could tell, the ice house was not a prosperous business. Moreover, it was 1957, and most folks in town owned Frigidaires. A few poor folks continued to use iceboxes, but there weren't a sufficient number of those to feed two men with unemployed wives.

I was getting nowhere with my mental jigsaw puzzle and boredom was beginning to set in when a car drove up I didn't recognize, but Tug obviously did. His elbow jabbed Hack in the ribs with such enthusiasm that Hack's hat almost fell off. Both men began moving faster and more cautiously than normal. I didn't recognize the man driving the black Buick, as he killed the engine and looked around to see if anyone was watching. I did the same. There was no one in sight except them and me. Tug and Hack knew me well and seemed unconcerned with a nine-year-old.

The man in the Buick had on a summer hat and sunglasses. He didn't leave the car. Hack went down the steps and to the passenger window, which was open for ventilation, laughed a patronizing laugh, talked a moment, then disappeared into the cooler. Tug stood by the cooler door as if on lookout. Less than half a minute later, Hack emerged with an ice bag about half full. As I looked closely, the edges of the sack were more square than round. It must have been lighter than a half block of ice because Hack easily handled it with one hand. With both Tug and Hack looking around numerous times, Hack quickly made his way to the passenger door, which the driver leaned over and opened so that Hack could place the bag on the floorboard. Hack looked around again as he counted the folding money and pocketed the cash. With a final nod, the driver sped off, a cloud of dust disguising his getaway. Hack and Tug nonchalantly returned to their perches.

My curiosity was piqued. I decided to make my move. After waiting an appropriate time I hopped down from the depot dock, walked to the single pair of shiny tracks, looked toward Evansville for the 2:00 train, and with no whistle or smoke in sight I balleted my way down the rails and jumped in front of the ice house.

"Hey, little man," Hack greeted.

"Hello, Mr. Hack," I responded.

"What's up?" Tug queried.

"Just waiting on the train. It looks like it may not make it."

"Oh, yeah, it'll make it. It just may not be today," Tug chuckled.

I climbed the wooden steps to the plank porch and sat down on one of the two dilapidated visitor chairs.

"Y'all got any cold Black Diamonds?" I asked, pretending not to know.

"You beeeet," Tug boasted, "one of the best crops in years. Bigger 'n I seen in ages and ice cold," he added in a salesman tone. "You wanna buy one, Cody?"

"I sure would like to. How much are they?"

"A penny a pound hot and two cents cold. How do you like 'em?" Tug grinned, wiping the sweat from his brow with his handkerchief.

"How much would a nice one cost, Tug?"

Tug eyed me with a look that could count the

nickels and dimes in my pocket, then winked an approval into my innocent eyes.

"I think we can make a deal," Tug encouraged. "How much you got?"

My mind raced through the calculation. Would it be worth the forty cents I had in my pocket to try and see what lay in the belly of the ice house? I decided quickly and reached into my pocket, pulling out a nickel, a dime, and a quarter, extending my open hand to Tug.

Tug ran a finger over my three coins, looking for more.

"Damn, boy, you drive a hard bargain," Tug nodded, belying his helplessness. Old Tug loved kids because he had none. I had him in my grasp.

He pulled the latch opening the chiller door. "I'll pick you out a nice one," he said as he headed into the cooler, meaning I should not come in. But I slipped in before the spring-loaded door closed, unbeknownst to Tug. The heavy door slammed shut. I stood quiet as a mouse, with the eyes of an owl. I hoped the dim bulb wouldn't go out as I scanned the cooler faster than a forty-acre watermelon patch. Only ice cold melons. There had to be more. Tug farted as he bent down to thump a medium-sized melon, which told me he didn't know I was inside.

My bare feet were beginning to stick to the floor like a tongue to an ice tray. I couldn't see my feet for the white smoke that lay like a cloud over the frozen wood floor. I sneaked behind Tug with the cunning of a panther.

There it was! Something that I had never seen

and definitely something that didn't belong. Behind carefully stacked blocks of ice was a stash of whiskey and beer. I suddenly realized my danger. Hack and Tug were bootleggers! Knowing I must not get caught, I silently made my way back to the door while Tug rummaged through his melons to pick me a nice one. Thank goodness he hadn't seen me. The door suddenly opened, and Hack stuck his irritated face in. Tug turned around, and I was caught in the crossfire of their sight.

"You know you ain't supposed to be in here, boy," Hack scolded.

"Yes, sir. I just wanted to see the melons," I replied sheepishly.

"Don't matter none. You get your butt outta here, boy," Hack blurted.

"He's okay, Hack," Tug said in sympathy and support. "I've knowed this boy all his life. Me and his granddaddy been knowing each other forever. He ain't done no harm."

Hack sucked his teeth in disgust as I headed for the door with my head down. "Okay, but don't let me catch you in here again," he said in a callous voice.

"No, sir, I won't," I said with just the right amount of shame and sincerity.

Tug carried my melon outside and set it on the porch, rubbing my head to brush away Hack's harshness. "That one look good enough to you, Cody?"

"Yes, sir, it's beautiful," I answered, noticing the chalked number 37 on the melon.

"It'll be perfect. Trust me." Tug winked.

I handed Tug my forty cents, which he pocketed

without counting, and I lifted the cold melon to my chest.

"Can you carry that, little man?"

"Yes, sir, I can make it."

I carefully descended the steps, cradling my purchase, eager to get away from Hack and thankful for Tug's inability to have children. The watermelon was freezing my arms, hands, and chest, but the pain was easily tolerated when I considered the option of being locked in the dark cooler until I froze to death.

I must have set the watermelon down fifteen times on my three-block walk home. I rested and thawed as I analyzed the bootlegging business.

For the first time everything made sense, even the times the ice house boys were inexplicably jailed. I now held the secret to the ice house, and it weighed a whole lot more than the watermelon. ❧

The Brown Bomber

*"Church in Turnip was enough to
scare the hell out of you."*

June brought the dreaded summer church revival,
claiming to dispense light. June also brought the fat,
juicy, brown June bug seeking light. I didn't know it
at the time, but the two were on a collision course.

The Church of Christ was located two blocks
from my house and one block from the courthouse.
The small stone building was spartan, with rows of
wooden pews and a baptistry located behind the elevated pulpit. The ceiling was low and flat with four
ceiling fans, eight screened windows, and two
plaques flanking the podium boasting the attendance, contributions, and hymn numbers of the day.
The air conditioning was furnished by God.

It was a Monday night in late June when Mother, my brother Jim, and I walked into the sweltering church. I was ten years old and missing my Little League game. I was not happy and, from the look of the congregation, no one else was either.

Church was three times a week for real Christians and less frequent for sinners. Revivals were once a year and eternally in June—seven nights of hellfire and damnation that simply couldn't be missed unless sickness or death were lurking. The mission of the Church of Christ was to save the Baptists, Methodists, and other misguided souls of Turnip.

Mother had prodded Jim and me into church thrice weekly since birth. Church was like an enema: if Mother thought we needed it, we got it. For me, the end results of the two were about the same.

The hard wooden pews were packed. There must have been 200 souls in attendance, forcing a good number to sit on folding chairs in the aisles. The windows were open, and light globes were glowing. Ceiling fans stirred the hundred-degree air mostly to the taller people. We shorter types were hypnotized with air from the cardboard stick fans our mother swished in our faces that displayed Jesus in a sunburst on one side and Hill's Lumber Hardware and Undertaking on the other.

Neckties were cinched up around white collars, and sweat was soaked up by white handkerchiefs. Chewing gum wrappers began to crinkle as mothers hoped the sweetness would distract the children from the ensuing sermon. I wondered if preachers got together and decided that forty-five minutes was the proper sermon length, or if God had written it in the Bible. The only thing I knew was, come hell or high water, the sermon was going to be at least forty-five minutes.

Excitement began to build in the congregation as we performed what must be the scripturally pre-scribed one song, one prayer, two songs, and the longer prayer. Then the out-of-town prophet rose from his front-row perch and ascended to the throne. I checked him out: big ears, long nose, fake smile backed with the teeth of a horse, beady eyes, black-rimmed glasses, red face, and a graying flat top that matched his suit. I didn't trust his smile because I knew hell was coming. But I didn't know everything that was coming.

The prophet's smile melted to a scowl as he began preaching. That was the last we saw of his front teeth. We saw plenty of his back teeth and ton-sils after that as the preacher alternated in shaking the Bible and pounding on the podium while orches-trating his voice from an enticing whisper to a threatening shout.

Being the ten-year veteran that I was, as soon as I got a bead on the preacher, I turned my attention to things of substance—the June bugs that had mis-takenly entered the double doors of the church look-ing for light. As the bugs banged from globe to globe, it seemed to me that the congregation and the bugs had entered the building with the same intentions and both were going to leave with the same feeling—a headache.

The big brown bugs buzzed louder, as did the preacher. Soon I heard only the bugs. I thought how dumb the silly things were when they could be in the fresh night air of the baseball field just three blocks away buzzing around the slick 1,000-watt bulbs rather than inside God's little oven. Nonetheless, I was glad they were here to entertain me.

Well, the bugs were smarter than I thought because they were soon trying to get out. They sounded like V-2 rockets over London as they roared overhead with all the speed they could muster before crashing full speed into walls. They hit with mighty thuds and fell to the floor, landing on their backs, each reaching upward like a baby with six arms. I decided to time them using Mother's watch to see how long it would take the poor bugs to get flipped over. After watching three minutes of relentless legwork by the June bug closest to me, I could not resist trying to help. I attempted a shoe offering to the little fella. Mother didn't embrace much leg motion, but she did embrace me with a strong arm around the neck and an ear-piercing whisper to sit still. So the bugs buzzed, thudded, squiggled, and crawled, looking for the same thing I did—the exit.

One June bug in particular will be forever in my memory. I always think of him as the "Brown Bomber." Maybe he was just a vindictive Baptist bug upset at finding himself trapped in a hot building with a screaming Church of Christ preacher. Regardless, he began to hit the wall more rapidly and with more intensity than I had ever seen. He was a one-man aerial show with a kamikaze heart.

It must have been forty minutes into the shouting when the preacher and the Brown Bomber gloriously met. The lathered-up preacher raised the Good Book and threw his head back, revealing only upper molars, when heaven arrived. In full flight and mid-sentence, the Brown Bomber smashed into the preacher's tonsils with a cavernous thud. The congregation gasped. My insides screamed with laughter as I slammed both hands over my mouth to muffle squeals. It was a perfect hit! My eyes were pouring water as I blinked hard to clear them, not wanting to miss anything.

The preacher disappeared from view, falling to his knees beside the podium, clutching his throat with both hands, while coughing and trying not to swallow. I couldn't resist standing up for a better view. The congregation tensed as empathetic coughs infected the room.

Then, with one vomitous cough, the preacher—now on all fours—brought up the Bomber. Two elders in the church rushed to the preacher's assistance, one slapping him on the back and the other offering a glass of water from the bathroom to wash down the Bomber's brown juice, I suppose.

I was almost peeing in my pants as I crossed my legs and struggled to restrain my glee.

I loved that bug! He had done what I had always wanted to do: *shut the preacher up*! The Brown Bomber was a martyr and my hero. His memorial was the glass of water that ever after adorned the podium ... that and my memory of his last mission.

Turner's Auto Electric

*"Turnip was a three church town with
one blinking yellow light."*

Tuesdays were normally uneventful days. But on this Tuesday morning there was electricity in the air.

Tom Turner had made an unwitting mistake on Monday afternoon. He decided to leave his son Tommy in charge of the family radio, TV, and auto parts store all day Tuesday while he drove the 150-mile round trip to Dallas to preview the latest in black and white televisions.

Turner's Auto Electric was located one store off the square facing the orange brick side wall of Dawson's Grocery with Highway 29 in between. It was a noisy part of town because the big trucks that stopped at Turnip's only blinking light had to rev their engines to struggle away from the stoplight.

Tom's store had a big, wide elevated sidewalk out front facing Highway 29, tall enough that you could sit on the edge and dangle your feet without hitting the pavement below. The sidewalk was shaded by a tin awning that extended well beyond the spit-and-whittle bench located directly in front of Tom's storefront window with "Turner's Auto Electric" proudly painted at adult eye level across the glass. Tom's storefront wasn't much wider than the parallel parking space in front of the store, with a half glass door secured by a hasp lock. The big glass display window extended from the ceiling to the top of the bench out front. Inside the window was a countertop where Tom displayed his wares, which ranged from radiator hoses and fan belts to beautifully shaped filament-filled glass tubes for radios and TVs. Tom's linoleum-covered cash register counter faced the door where Tom greeted everyone who entered with a big false teeth smile and a nasal "How ya doin'?" The counter was located a sufficient distance from the door and display to allow several customers to stand at the counter while Tom fetched parts from the four lanes of wood shelving, permitting Tom and the customers to keep an eye on each other. Haste was not a part of Tom's routine as he fumbled from box to box in the dimly lit store, raising and lowering his bifocals from his forehead to his nose. As Tom awaited customers at the register, he had a perfect view of both the walking and driving traffic as well as the backs of the white-haired heads sitting out front on the bench. The heads bobbed and weaved in rhythm with the flow of traffic.

Tom was a large man, a full head taller than my dad, with short-cropped gray hair groomed into a flat top so perfect that it required no Butch Wax. He spoke in a whine that seemed to come more from his nose than his mouth. His talk was slow and deliberate, perfectly matching his patience. He allowed his customers to come behind the counter and help him find parts, which they usually did with more speed than Tom.

Tom's store was exciting. It was the only electronics store in town. Tom had come to that quite by accident. People who had come in for years for car parts also needed radio and TV parts. As he expanded his operation, he needed help. So he hired quiet, frail Sparky Wells to repair radios and TVs.

Sparky was always fidgeting and soldering radio and TV chassis and testing and replacing tubes. The rear of Tom's store, where Sparky worked with its electronic squeaks and squalls, sounded like a late night tomcat fight. Sparky was a thin man with a wedge-shaped face and a curving bird's beak nose. He had red hair and skinny fingers that fidgeted. His voice was so soft the customers hated to ask him questions about his repairs for fear he would either cry or run and hide. He always stayed at the back of Tom's shop at his small, well-lighted workbench, where no one bothered him except us kids. We had to slip in the back door of Tom's and talk in a whisper if we wanted to visit with Sparky. Otherwise Tom would run us out for bothering his help. Sparky was nice to us and had a surprising sense of humor and a glint in his eye that went unnoticed to most of his customers and certainly to Tom. We were not customers. We were helpers.

The entire back wall of the store was piled to the ceiling with deceased radio chassis, TV parts, and picture tubes. Television was a new invention, and most sets didn't work well. The picture was either fuzzy or rolling, or there was sound with no picture or picture with no sound.

Sparky had the best trash bin in town located below his workbench, where he kept all sorts of old parts. Tom wouldn't let Sparky throw anything away. The bin was full of inventive possibilities. There were magnets with yards and yards of bright copper wire wrapped around them, tubes glowing with brilliant shades of orange and blue, and knobs and dials for every occasion. We had puttered with Sparky's no-good parts for endless hours and never had an invention to work until this particular day.

Jim and I strolled into the store around midmorning on that particular Tuesday. Summer was less than half over. Tom was gone to Dallas. Sparky was fixing, just as diligently as if Tom had been in the store, and Tom's only son, Tommy, heir to the store, was left in charge for the whole day. Tommy had told us the day before that for the first time he was running the store while his dad was gone. Tommy's ambivalence about the honor was evident in his body language, because he would have to man the counter all day while Jim and I exercised our summer freedom. Thus the invitation to visit the store.

As Jim opened the screen door and we stepped inside, Tommy had a proud look about himself because of both the responsibility his dad had placed in his hands and for suddenly seeing himself elevated above his peers. Even though Tommy was only thirteen, the same as Jim and three years older than me, he was trying to act much older.

I wasn't sure what opportunities the day held and what problems might develop as a result of Tommy's being the boss. We might help Sparky smoke solder or look for buffalo nickels and Indian head pennies in the register or sit on the tall concrete curb out front and count tires on the eighteen-wheelers. Twenty-two tires were unusual, thirty-two only occurred every couple of weeks, and only once in my entire life had I spotted a rig with forty-two tires.

We hopped up on the countertop and made ourselves at home. It was our first subtle test of Tommy's authority. When he took no position on our assertiveness, I knew it was going to be a good day. As usual, there were not many customers to bother us. We visited and snooped in all the shelves as people leisurely came and went, with Tommy doing a good job of finding parts and making change from the register. He had often helped his dad after school and on Saturdays, but never had he been entrusted with the entire responsibility of the store.

As Tommy waited on Mr. Orsborn, my rummaging brought me to a strange object—round and about three feet long, with two prongs on the end like that of a fluorescent light tube. In electric red letters on the side it said "Hot Shot." I couldn't figure out its purpose, so I took it to the front of the store where Jim and Tommy were sitting and asked, "Hey, Tommy, what's this for?"

Tommy's eyes lit up as he said with a straight face and a suspicious amount of interest, "Come here and I'll show you."

As Tommy knew, little brothers are leery of older brothers and older brothers' friends who are eager to share knowledge. I stood my ground and said, "Naw, just tell me what it does."

Tommy firmed his neck and voice and said in an adult tone, "I can't tell you, but I can show you."

He looked more believable than not, and my curiosity outweighed my better judgment, so I handed it to Tommy and asked again, "So what does it do?"

He stated in a believable tone, "It's a vibrator."

I should have known better, but I took the bait. "Well, show me how it feels," I said. I had always liked the feel of Daddy's hand-held vibrator that he rubbed on my back, neck, and head.

Tommy said, "This thing feels great. Stick out your leg and I'll show you." I measured his eyes and hesitantly extended my right leg. Tommy gently pressed the two prongs against my skin just below my shorts. Simultaneously Tommy twisted the handle, jabbed the prongs in deeper, and contorted his face into that of a mad scientist with sadistic laughter. A jolt of electricity shot through my leg from the tips of my toes and up to the top of my head. I had just been unforgettably introduced to a cattle prod whose three-foot cylinder was filled with a fresh supply of high-powered batteries. Tommy and Jim roared with laughter at my gullibility. My scream even brought Sparky Wells out of hiding. Everyone seemed to delight in my pain.

I hadn't felt anything like it since the time I crawled around the back of our TV to see what was wrong and touched the wires, getting myself knocked back into the wall with the electricity evidencing itself most pointedly in the silver fillings of my teeth. I didn't laugh then, and I wasn't laughing now. Little brothers seemed to have been created for things like this.

We chased each other around the store for a while with the hot shot until Sparky sheepishly reminded Tommy that his dad might not approve of our conduct. Tommy was persuaded and said we needed to return the hot shot to its rightful location. We compromised, deciding to lay it on the counter where we could still touch it.

I was the only one who had received a full jolt, and that dismayed me. As my mind began to accelerate, considering possible torture subjects, it became evident that probably no one else would be as stupid and trusting as me. Then I had a flash. A trap!

I blurted, "Hey guys, let's find a way to set a trap for someone and then zap 'em!"

Coming to life, Jim and Tommy looked at each other in appreciation of my idea. Three small minds began to whirl. Before long, Tommy realized that we could connect strands of Sparky's fine copper to each pole of the prod and strike at a greater distance. We considered wiring our friend's bike, but Tommy couldn't leave the store. We thought about wiring

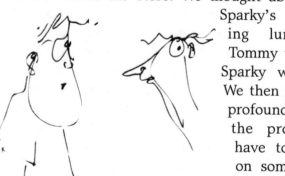

Sparky's chair during lunch, but Tommy was afraid Sparky would tell. We then fell on the profound idea that the prod would have to be used on someone who would never know who the executioner was. We deduced they would have to be dumb, which meant they

would either be very young or very old. Very old had two advantages: there was an abundant supply, and they generally had poor eyesight. We were impressed with our ingenuity.

Simultaneously, we turned our heads to look at the front picture window just as an old man sat on the bench out front to watch the auto and pedestrian traffic—all the components for the perfect crime. Now thoughts and words had to be made flesh.

We didn't hesitate. We rushed back to Sparky's bin and went through discarded rolls of copper wire until we found the perfect gauge, scarcely larger than a hair. The spit-and-whittle bench would be the electric chair. Two fine wires would be laid four inches apart and across the entire seat of the bench. The wires would be wrapped around the doorjamb, taped along the wall, and attached to the hot shot below Tom's sales counter, thereby requiring no movement from the executioner. The weapon would never be seen, yet the victim was in perfect view.

Our hearts raced with excitement. Thankfully, the old man on the bench didn't sit long. We had fretted that he might fall asleep. As soon as he was gone, and the coast was clear, we set the trap. In less than ten minutes, without Sparky's suspecting a thing, Tommy Turner, heir to the throne, had unwittingly made a career decision.

We giggled, tingled, and waited for what seemed an eternity. Finally, two old geezers sat themselves down on the bench, and we looked at each other, hardly able to contain our bodily fluids, and ducked behind the counter for a strategy session. Tommy said, "We can't shoot two of 'em or they'll know somethin's fishy." We exchanged glances and nodded in agreement.

"We'll have to wait 'til one leaves," Jim reluctantly replied. We rose above the counter with innocent faces. We could see the shoulders and white heads of the old men in intricate detail, for they were no more than eight feet in front of us, separated by a secure-feeling piece of plate glass. The old fellas must have talked and spat and scratched and farted for the better part of an hour as they watched folks pass. Then finally one stood up, shook hands with his compadre, and departed.

That left but one duck on the pond. Our perfect number. And as the Lord would have it, that one was none other than Hobby Sterns—old, white-headed, high-spirited, half-blind, and mostly crazy. We waited a couple of minutes that were every bit as energy-charged as that amount of time on Christmas morning from waking up until the first package was unwrapped. We could wait no longer. We looked at each other and nodded. Tommy shot the juice!

It was everything we had imagined and more. Old Hobby lurched forward with a jerk and a hurtful holler like he had been stabbed in the butt with a knife. He looked like a dancing puppet on a string until Tommy untwisted the hot shot. Our laughter was confined to our chests, realizing more than that would betray us.

Hobby continued to jerk, then grabbed his heart, slumping on the bench. Old Hobby might have lived through World War I, but we had brought him to his knees on that old bench. He thought he was having a heart attack as he waved for Hack McGee to come

from across the street and help. Hack came at a run,
and naturally we went outside to assist.

"You all right, Hobby?" No reply. "What's
wrong?" asked Hack in a frightened voice.

"Don't know," came the breathy reply from old
Hobby. "I think I'm havin' a heart attack, but I ain't
shore. Sumpin' jus hit me . . . like a sharp pain."

I struggled to hold my laughter in. It was just like
containing one of those church giggles that wanted
out so badly but could not at any cost be permitted
to exit. I coughed and turned my head. All eyes were
on Hobby as a couple of other folks joined us.

"Hobby, you want me to call Jimmy Dale to bring
the ambulance?" asked Hack in a confused tone.

"Naw. Not jus yet. Let me jus set a while and see
if it hits me again."

I could have answered that one for him.
Smugness overcame us.

Tommy asked in an adult and most believable
tone, "Is there anything we can do, Mr. McGee?"

"Naw. Thanks, boys. We'll jus set a while and see
if he gets to feelin' better."

After a bit old Hobby began to sit straight on the
bench and regained some of his color and composure. I could tell he was aware that his ass was what
was hurting more than his heart, but he clearly had
no clue as to what had hit him. I breathed easier as
I realized old Hobby wasn't going to die on us and
that Jimmy Dale wasn't going to come racing up in
the ambulance with the siren screaming.

After a while old Hobby had pulled himself together and decided he'd best head on home. "If I'm
gonna die, it's gonna be in my own bed and not on

some goddamned old hot sidewalk." Hack helped him to his feet as old Hobby steadied himself, rubbing his ass through his striped overalls, and slowly began to walk to the corner blinking light with Hack at his side.

The crowd disbursed and we returned inside, simultaneously ducking down behind the counter and laughing until our necks hurt and tears came from our eyes. We had finally evened the score with old Hobby for spitting at and on our bare feet as we danced past his bench. He was a contrary old man who enjoyed his humor at another's expense. We recounted the highlights of the episode in a combination of laughter and speech that was only discernible to one who had been there.

Our common old Tuesday was taking shape. We regained our composure with bloodshot eyes and discussed our options. The only course of action that seemed plausible was a reenactment.

Foolishly, we waited.
Another duck landed.
A solo. But as God would have it, he wasn't as senile as old Hobby.

It was Walter Hornsby, a quiet, hardworking farmer.

Not a regular downtowner. He was just resting a few minutes while Bob Dunley, next door, loaded cattle feed on his old pickup out front.

We were set. Our triumph had affected our judgment. Jim and I nodded, and Tommy shot him the juice.

He jumped from the bench and grabbed his ass. "Goddamn, what the hell is goin' on?" he blurted out in a hurt voice, anger building in his neck and face. Things didn't look good. We dropped down behind the counter with frightened giggles.

Bob Dunley came to the bench and said, "What's the matter, Walter?"

"Damned if I know, but somethin' on that goddamned bench stung the hell outta me."

As I peeked over the counter, my heart sank as two pairs of younger-than-anticipated eyes scrutinized the bench.

"What the hell are these two wires?" Walter asked in a harsh, red-faced tone.

"Hell if I know," Bob stated as he began to trace them.

As they turned toward the doorjamb, the men looked up and recognized the guilt on three young faces.

"What the hell have you boys done?" Walter shouted, staring us in the eye.

We were had. There was only one option, and Tommy the proprietor took it—confess with a lie.

"Mr. Hornsby, we hooked up this here hot shot to these two wires to try to shock some of our friends and it accidentally went off on you."

"Goddamn it to hell, boy. Don't lie to me," the normally soft-spoken farmer said.

I knew we were going to die. I kept quiet and Jim added, "We sure are sorry, Mr. Hornsby. We didn't intend to shock you. It was an accident." Jim sounded pretty convincing.

Hornsby didn't buy a word of it.

"Let me tell you something, Mr. Tom Turner Junior. Me and yore daddy are gonna have a talk. Where is he?"

"He's in Dallas, sir, and may not be back for quite some time." Another good lie, I thought.

About that time, Sparky Wells edged his way around the corner and took a stand I'll never forget nor be able to repay.

"Mr. Hornsby," he firmly stated, "I'm responsible for these boys. I know they didn't mean no harm. I'll take care of this for you, and I'll talk to Mr. Turner. I'll see these boys get what they got comin'. You can count on it."

Mr. Hornsby's anger receded only slightly. "All right, Sparky, you see that you take care of this mess proper." I sighed inside. He pointed at each one of us as he began to leave. "If you boys try *anything* like this again, I'm gonna skin your asses! You hear me?" His voice rose, "Skin your asses!"

"Yes, sir," came the simple unisoned reply.

He left and we lived. Sparky had saved us.

As Sparky turned to walk back to his workbench, he softly said, "That ought to be enough for today, boys."

He never mentioned the episode to Mr. Turner. Nor did we. 🦋

Sleepwalking

"Why couldn't I have had girls?"

I was awakened in the middle of the night by what sounded like water being poured from a tea kettle. All the lights were off. I looked at my alarm clock—3:15. I looked at my older brother Jim's twin bed. He was gone!

I quietly hopped off the bed, my feet hitting the cold wood floor. I followed the noise past the family bathroom. I couldn't imagine what was going on.

I flipped the kitchen light switch, and there was Jim, peeing in the empty metal trashcan. He never acknowledged the light or me.

Flipping the light off, I sneaked back to bed, assuming Daddy's snore kept Mother from investigating. I pulled the covers to my chin and waited in the dark. A few minutes later, Jim wandered back to our room and lay down in his bed without a word.

Jim and I awoke the next morning to the sound of Mother's irritated voice as she stood in our doorway.

"Who did this?" She was holding the newly elected toilet.

"Did what?" Jim asked in his morning voice.

Mother turned to me and fumed, "Andrew Cody, is this your idea of a joke?"

"No, ma'am." I looked at Jim and decided to give him up. "Mother, Jim was sleepwalking again," I said matter of factly.

"My word!" Mother added, exiting with the sloshing trashcan extended at arm's length. "Why couldn't I have had girls?"

Titanic Bill

*"Don't pay them no mind, boy.
They ain't never been nowhere."*

Bill Dubes was a legend that I had never seen in person. He lived in my grandfather's stories, and I did not know if he were fact or fiction. Bill only came to town once a year, but when he did, everyone knew. It was a crisp Saturday morning in November when I met Bill for the first and only time. I was eight years old.

It was a time when people in Turnip were buying their first television sets and beginning to relax from the pain and scarcity of World War II. Bill was not one of those people.

I was sitting on the low concrete wall that elevated the courthouse above all other buildings on the square when I first sighted Bill. I knew it could only be Bill because of the pictures my grandfather had painted in my mind.

Bill was standing tall in a wooden wagon, driving a team of mules, with his spotted dog at attention on

67

the wooden seat beside him. The old wagon had sideboards on three sides and rolled along on spoked wooden wheels. Bill's wild white hair was blowing in the breeze as he popped the leather reins, navigating the mules around the downtown cars that were attempting to get out of Bill's way. "Get up there, Ned. Gee a little bit there, Jeb," Bill commanded as he uneasily steered the wagon to a stop in front of Dawson's Grocery, where I had never seen anything other than a car or truck park.

I made my way closer as Bill tied the reins and climbed down from the wagon. He instructed his attentive dog to stay put and rubbed and talked to each mule, attempting to settle them in their foreign surroundings.

He approached the bench in front of Dawson's, and the old-timers stood to shake hands. They smiled, obviously pleased to see that a part of their earlier life continued to exist. Bill was dressed in striped overalls covering well-worn long handles buttoned to the top. Beneath his wilted and sweat-stained gray hat hung waist-length white hair down both sides of his head. You could hardly tell if Bill was coming or going. Between his hat and beard was a pair of piercing blue eyes as wild as his hair. His leathery skin looked to be a hundred years old, as did the huge revolver strapped to his hip.

I kept my distance but stayed within earshot of the conversation. "Hello, boys." Bill shook each hand earnestly.

"How's thangs in them hills, Bill?" asked Hobby Sterns, probably eighty years old himself.

"Fair to middlin'," Bill replied cheerfully.

"Killed any bear up there lately, Bill?" Hobby mused.

"Oh, yeah," Bill said loudly. He looked around and spotted me. "Killed a ten-foot-tall griz just last week," Bill added soberly.

"That right?" Hobby said, looking my direction.

Bill nodded, then said, "Well, I got to get a few possibles and head outta town afore these city folk run me over with onna them fancy automobiles." He tipped his hat to Hobby and the boys and eyeballed me as he turned toward Dawson's front door.

I gathered my courage. There was a question I was dying to know the answer to. Realizing my opportunities were limited, I managed, "Hello, Bill." That stopped him in his tracks as we stood face to beard.

"Howdy, little fella," Bill quipped. "Do I know you?"

"No, sir," I replied shyly. "But you know my grandfather. I'm Hooker Woodson's grandson, Cody." That brought a gleam to his eye and I presumed a smile to his face, although I couldn't see it. He extended his wrinkled hand for a shake. I hesitantly gripped the strong paw.

"Hooker Woodson. Well, what do you know? How's old Hooker adoin'?" he asked mischievously.

"Just fine, sir. He's doing just fine." I struggled for conversation before my big question.

"You tell Hooker that Titanic

Bill says hey," Bill replied as he began to move to the grocery door, turning to check his team and his dog.

"I sure will, Mr. Bill . . . but before you go, can I ask you something, sir?"

"Sure, boy, ask away," Bill bellowed.

"Well, sir, I was wondering if," I hesitated, "if it was true that you were on the *Titanic*?"

Bill's wild eyes opened larger, and he became dead serious as he asked, "Who told you I was on the *Titanic*?" I was uneasy talking to the scary old-timer, but I wanted to hear for myself if what my grandfather had told me was true. He, like Bill, was known to invest in tall tales.

"Well, sir, my grandfather told me." I readied myself to move back or run if need be.

"Well, then," Bill said, squatting down to meet me eye-to-eye, "I sure was!" Then he began in a once-upon-a-time tone, "It was a cold, dark night when we hit that berg. . . ." His eyes captured mine. "Smacked it head on," he exclaimed, hitting one fist into the other, "and then that big bucket of bolts started a sinkin'!" His eyes twinkled, not having had this kind of audience for a while. I was focused on the tobacco stains dripping down his white beard where the words were coming out when I heard the spit-and-whittle boys begin to snicker. Recapturing my attention with more volume and passion, Bill continued, "Well, people were a-screamin' and a-jumpin' on lifeboats and I said to myself 'Hell, I'll just swim for it.' That's when I grabbed two loaves of bread floating by and stuck one under each arm and swam to shore. When I got to shore I fought a bear for forty days and forty nights. Damn near kilt me, but I finally got the best of 'im." With that, the boys next to us broke out in knee-slapping laughter.

Bill soberly turned to them, and they quieted. Then he turned back to me, placing his hand on my shoulder, and said, "Don't pay them no mind, boy. They ain't never been nowhere." With that he turned and entered the store. I was spellbound.

Half an hour later, after loading six sacks of groceries in the wagon, Bill climbed to the seat and his waiting dog, untied the reins, turned to me, and said, "Boy, you ask Hooker if he and the Indian have found the treasure on Lost Hill yet." With a roar of laughter, Titanic Bill turned and spanked the mules while sucking kisses to them. He gave me a wave without looking back.

Three Masked Men

"We scanned the crime scene one more time.
Not a creature was stirring."

Idle minds were definitely the devil's workshop for three adolescent boys, as my brother Jim, our friend Tommy, and I planned a surprise attack for the following morning. I was ten years old and Jim and Tommy were thirteen. Our target was fourteen-year-old Gary Dibble, the principal's son.

Gary lived near downtown, a block from Jim and me and two blocks from Tommy. The four of us were best friends, and Gary's house was our hangout. The planned attack originated in the fertile mind of Tommy Turner, the biggest kid in town for his age, but not the brightest.

We envisioned a midnight attack, but our mothers' curfews and watchful eyes made that impossible, so a predawn strike the following morning would have to do. It was mid-July and warm, and there were no streetlights as the three of us met in my front yard in the pitch-black early morning to execute the caper. Only a smattering of porch lights in the neighborhood were on, with a few people milling around inside their dimly lit houses readying for the day. We talked in excited whispers as we met on the street corner.

"Have you got the water guns, Tommy?" Jim asked.

"Yeah!" Tommy replied as he passed out the three guns heavy with water.

"Did you get the stockings?" Tommy asked.

"Yeah, here they are!" Jim pulled three of Mother's stockings from his back pocket.

The first thought of an unpleasant consequence crossed my mind. *I wonder if Mother will miss those?*

We pulled the nylon stockings over our heads and down to our necks, squinting to see if we were recognizable. Unable to see in the darkness, we giggled as we felt the deformed features of each other's faces.

"We're gonna scare the daylights out of Gary!" I observed.

"Yeah, it's gonna be great!" Tommy exclaimed. "He's gonna think we're *The Creature from the Black Lagoon.*"

We began stumbling the one block toward Gary's house, unable to see much through the thick nylons that pressed against our eyelashes.

"I gotta take this dang thing off," Jim said, wrestling the stocking from his head. I had forgotten he was claustrophobic. Tommy and I followed suit.

We were in a giggly mood and a sneaky crouch as we rounded the corner and saw Gary's porch and room. The house was dark. Gary didn't have a dog to warn him, and his wide-open double hung windows beckoned us. Gary's room had a screen door next to the two big windows that opened to his porch.

We were no more than a step away from the porch when Tommy stopped us with a raised hand. We could see Gary lying shirtless on the twin bed under a white sheet—serene and irresistible. Tommy pointed to the ground beside the wooden porch steps, and our minds tingled with the same vision: a neatly coiled garden hose connected to a faucet lay next to the steps. We simultaneously nodded and stuck the water guns in our pockets, hardly able to control the thrill inside us. Tommy bent down and whispered in my ear, "When I give you the signal, turn on the faucet full blast!" I nodded and a piece of giggle slipped from my mouth. I quickly covered it with my hand.

We scanned the crime scene one more time. Not a creature was stirring. We pulled on our masks, and Tommy gently picked up the end of the water hose. Jim and Tommy tiptoed barefoot onto the wooden porch, taking flanking positions at the window. Between them I could see Gary's face turned toward us with his eyes shut, and his outstretched arm resting on the windowsill. He looked so peaceful.

I jerked with emotion, keeping one hand over my mouth as I crouched beside the faucet. Tommy looked at me and slowly raised his hand. Then, like a guillotine, his hand dropped and I twirled the valve open. The hose began to jump. Tommy's thumb was over the end, adding pressure to the coming spray. When the water hit his thumb we all screamed as loudly as we could as the cold water blasted Gary, Gary's bed, Gary's furniture, and Gary's floor. The impact was beyond my wildest vision.

Gary jumped out of the bed in terror. As he leaped onto the linoleum floor, now awash, he fell with a huge thud. "Who's there? Who are you?" he screamed from the floor. Mr. and Mrs. Dibble's light came on, as did his sister Gwen's in the next room. Unfortunately, there was now enough light for identification.

Simultaneously, we realized our peril. Tommy threw down the gushing water hose, and we ran like the wind. Unfortunately, I was the slowest breeze. In no time we heard the voice of Principal Dibble. "Tommy Turner, you get back here! Jim and Cody, you get back here, too! I mean now!"

We wouldn't have stopped for God Almighty. In full flight, headed for Tommy's garage, we rounded the corner and yanked off our masks. We stood inside the one-car garage breathing hard, not saying a word. Our eyes darted from face to face, hoping for a miracle. None came. We didn't know whether to laugh or cry. We finally decided the best idea was to return to the scene of the crime and beg forgiveness before our parents were called.

At that moment, we heard the phone ring in Tommy's house. We looked at each other and Jim said, "We gotta go home, Tommy. See ya later."

Jim turned and ran with me on his heels as Tommy pleaded in loud whispers, "Don't leave me! Come back, you cowards! You're in this, too!"

The three masked men had to face Mrs. Dibble that afternoon. With Gary's bedding on the clothes-line, the floor mopped, and Gary's mattress draped over the porch swing, Mrs. Dibble tongue-lashed us mercilessly as we three looked at the ground. Jim and I had already been lashed by Daddy. Tommy's parents didn't believe in spanking.

It would be a long time before Jim and I would take part in another of Tommy's harebrained schemes. And none of the future plans would involve the principal's house. 🧩

A Trip to Dewey's

*"If you're a real man and not
a lily-livered coward . . ."*

There was a sure-fire way to tell if you were a tough guy in Turnip. But you had to wait for mid-July. Mid-July, when you couldn't play outside in the heat of the day unless you stayed in the shade for fear of getting polio. Mid-July, when the cars would drive down the narrow, small town streets and you couldn't hear the engine for the sound of the bottoms of the wide white sidewall tires sticking to the pavement.

It was one of those blistering afternoons that my best friend Ben and I chose to prove our manhood. Ben was my brother's age, three years older than me, with reddish-blond wavy hair, freckles, and thick glasses. He was tough as a boot and smarter than anybody I knew.

Ben had escaped after lunch from his mom, easily as usual. My escape required more planning. Mother thought it unwise to let children run and play in the heat because only last year one of her high school students had gotten polio from what was feared to be overexposure to the sun. He was still in the hospital in an iron lung.

Summer afternoons at our house were reserved for naps, preceded by a story that Mother would read aloud to my brother Jim and me as the three of us lay side by side in the bed with a book out-stretched above us. Jim would follow the words in the book; I could only identify the page numbers. Mother would usually slip away after we were asleep, leaving only the cool breeze from the attic fan being pulled gently across our shirtless bodies.

We lived in a white frame house one block from the courthouse square and one block from the school. Our house sat on a large corner lot sur-rounded by eleven huge pecan trees which permitted the native Bermuda grass to only grow in splotches. We had two bedrooms, one for Mother and Daddy and one for Jim and me, which Jim called his room. We had one bathroom, and it had a waiting line.

The house was comfortable and comparable to others in town. We were accustomed to sweating in the summer and walking on cold floors in the winter. Only a few people in Turnip could afford wall-to-wall carpet or air-conditioners. The yard was my main concern: it had plenty of cool shade and enough grass to play football on, a clubhouse that the neighborhood boys had helped us build, which was continually being remodeled, a basketball goal in a semi-circular area that had been pounded on so much that grass would never grow, enough concrete sidewalk for skidding our bicycle tires on or for writing on with chalk, a one-car garage which leaned to the west and wobbled when we climbed on its roof, and a three-wire clothesline for Mother's washing. Our house was situated a comfortable distance from our neighbors but close enough to call our friends with a holler.

When Ben knocked on the door of our house, inviting me to come out and play, I saw the perturbed expression on Mother's face. Most of our friends knew Mother's rules, but Ben didn't, having recently returned to Turnip from Guam. Ben was a self-proclaimed Air Force brat who recognized authority and the opportunity to avoid it. That was also obvious to Mother. Nonetheless, we pled our case for making a short trip to Dewey's Filling Station, to which Mother surprisingly relented and allowed me to go but not Jim. This was a reward for my having sustained an early morning BB gun blast to the leg from Jim as I hid under the kitchen table. After a stern lecture stipulating that we walk slowly and stay in the shade, acknowledged by cross-my-heart-and-hope-to-die, off we went. Ben was careful not to slam the screen door on the way out. He smiled a self-serving smile, to which Mother replied by raising an eyebrow.

Once outside I removed my hand from my pants pocket, revealing my crossed fingers. Ben could lie, but I couldn't, at least not without justification.

We walked slowly toward the front yard, hopping so as not to step on a piece of sunshine and catch polio. We were both relieved when we rounded the corner and were out of range of Mother's omniscient kitchen window. There we were, free at last, standing in the front yard, digging our toes in the cool sandy soil between the strips of St. Augustine grass Mother had made Jim and me plant the week before as punishment for a Monopoly game free-for-all.

Ben and I were dressed pretty much the same as all the other kids in this town of 381 people—barefoot, short pants, and a shirt. Usually my shirt was one of Mother's homemade flour sack shirts—the ones with collars too long or too short, pockets too high or too low, adorned with whatever buttons happened to be in the drawer of the Singer. Mother said only "heathen children" would be seen in public without a shirt. I was more concerned with the pants myself—the direction the zipper faced, whether it was up or down, and if the seat had been ripped out and might expose my backside.

As I walked across the yard half a step behind Ben, he passed curiously close to the trunk of our largest pecan tree. He immediately ducked behind it, yanking me with him. I looked up to see what he had on his mind.

Crouched behind the tree, Ben looked me straight in the eye through thick glasses which made his eyes appear smaller than they actually were. His expression was serious as he said, "Now here's the deal, kid. If you're a real man and not a lily-livered coward, you gotta walk from here to Dewey's Filling Station without getting off the pavement. You can't run, you can't step in the shade—not even for a second—and you can only walk in the blackest, gooeyest part of the street." I dared to glance from Ben's eyes to the street, only to grimace at the sight of heat squiggles rising from the tar and rock surface like a desert mirage. I swallowed. Ben continued, "If a car is comin' you got to make him go around you or let him run over you, because you can't get out of the road. If you do, you ain't no man, you're a chicken."

I acknowledged the rules with a nod to Ben. My conscience thought about Mother; my ego, about manhood. Ego won. We peeked once more to be sure Mother wasn't looking, and into the street we went. I knew Ben was tough enough to do it. I only hoped that I had enough dirt and calluses on the bottoms of my feet to make the two-block walk.

As we stepped onto the street, pain soon overcame any further thoughts of Mother. Ben set the pace, and it couldn't have been slower. The black goop attached itself to the bottoms of my feet like molten flypaper. As I looked over my shoulder, I could actually see my tracks in the pools of asphalt with little points sticking up in the tar where it had attached to my skin. Panic was not far away.

I turned my head forward and looked down. Surprisingly, my toes were still there. I vowed not to look again. When Ben wasn't watching, I would rotate my weight to each part of my foot for cooling while trying to keep my balance. When Ben did look, I was quick to be flat-footed and emotionless.

Sweat was rolling off our faces. Each step got hotter and hotter, and Ben seemed to go slower and slower, but I wasn't about to say anything. I knew that once each summer was all it took to prove my manhood, and that every kid who didn't want to be a coward had to make the same walk.

After almost a block, with only Judge Forbes' big Oldsmobile slowly veering around us, half in the road and half in the ditch, I began to see the old wooden Coke boxes stacked at the rear of Dewey's Gulf Station. The pain had now stabilized. Almost unbearable, but stable. Ben never flinched, and I managed to refrain from screaming. Finally we stepped onto the cracked, oil-stained concrete of Dewey's single-bay station and into its shade.

Dewey was in his customary position, sitting on a propped-up wooden Coke box, his belly completely hiding his belt, chewing his tobacco, and talking with his black helper, Lester. Dewey smiled as he saw us coming. He gave us the quick once over, stopping his inspection at our feet. With a grin he said, "It's a scorcher out there, ain't it, boys?"

"Yes, sir," we replied in unison. Of course we didn't let Dewey and Lester know about our accomplishment. That would not have been manly. We simply looked at each other with eye language that acknowledged that we were in fact men—and tough men at that. 🐾

A Bird in the Hand

*"I was about to shoot a gun . . .
and take a big, innocent life."*

Old man Riley was the half blind and mostly deaf owner of the Turnip Dry Goods Store situated catty-cornered from the courthouse. Six days a week at closing time, he would fire up his black humpback Chevy, keeping his foot on the accelerator until the engine screamed and vibrated enough for him to know the car was running. With smoke boiling from the rear of the car, Mr. Riley—a double grip on the steering wheel and looking straight ahead—would back directly onto Highway 79 across both lanes, stopping just short of the ditch before lurching forward on his way home. Everyone in Turnip knew his routine and appreciated the smoke signal. Locals customarily paused in unison to see if the old man would back over some foreigner in a car approaching Turnip's blinking light. Tires and horns screeched often, but if Mr. Riley ever heard them, he never let on.

I didn't care for Mr. Riley's Dry Goods Store. The store and the name reflected his personality. Dry. He had no interest in fraternizing with a boy, probably realizing he wouldn't live long enough to see me as a paying customer. He shooed me out of his store a couple of times for fingering the merchandise, and that told me all I needed to know about him. But I suppose that also piqued my interest in targeting him for a measured dose of mischief.

Old man Riley and I had one love in common: birds. He loved to raise them, and I loved to shoot them. I suppose that put us on the fateful course.

I prized my Daisy BB gun. All my spare change from rummaging Coke bottles out of the ditches was spent on ammunition. A dime would go a long way in the '50s, and I was the king of stretch. After exchanging Coke bottles for cash at Dewey's Filling Station, I would cross the two lanes and enter Mrs. Hill's Hardware Store to purchase as many packets of copper BBs as my money would allow. I would twist open the hole in the top of the barrel, pour the BBs in my mouth, and spit them into the gun, losing none—provided I didn't swallow. The aftertaste was bitter but afforded a couple of good spitballs. Spitting was big in Turnip. In fact, it was considered an art form. I'd seen the old-timers on the spit-and-whittle benches pummel many a scurrying bare foot as it passed their gallery.

Leaving the hardware store, my gun heavy with BBs, my pulse quickened as I considered my new target. Mr. Riley had the only pigeons in town and beauties they were, often perching like standing dominoes on the peak of his tin-roofed barn adjacent to his house. Mr. Riley's two-story white house, in need of paint, was only a couple of blocks from town. I had walked past his house and barn many times and studied his pigeons. The barn beside his house was the favorite perch for the big fat birds. They were always there, just sitting, completely irresistible. He fed and loved pigeons. I saw and loved opportunity.

It was a Wednesday afternoon. I assumed old man Riley was minding the store as my BB gun and I made our way into the peach orchard and to the wood railing fence that surrounded his barn. I crouched, clearing the weeds to the side, and counted seven pigeons on the roof. A lucky number. They were beautifully colored and didn't seem to mind my presence. My pulse quickened, and for the first time I felt a tinge of conscience at the thought of killing a bird so beautiful and so tame. I blinked my conscience away.

The birds didn't budge as I dropped to one knee, raising my barrel and propping it on the middle rail of the plank fence for a steady aim. Carefully looking side to side, with no sign of Mr. Riley, I quietly cocked the gun and selected a big fat white target with pink legs. I lowered my head to the peep site, taking dead aim, and slowly squeezed the trigger. The gun kicked, and I watched the BB curve downward, hitting the tin roof with a loud *ping*. I cringed. The birds instantly flew away, flapping fearfully.

I pulled the gun back to my side and awaited their return. After several minutes they were circling the barn and hesitantly they began to land on the ridge again. One, two, three, landed. Then four, five,

six, and finally seven. Still lucky, I thought.
Remaining on my right knee and again placing the
gun through the fence rails, I pulled the stock to my
shoulder. Without looking around, I eased my head
to the peep site again and closed one eye.

The white bird was about to meet his maker
when a large, strong hand from nowhere cupped
over my left shoulder. I jumped as if shot and looked
up in fear. It was my worst nightmare—Mr. Riley. He
bent toward me with a pigeon perching on his left
index finger. I fell back on my hands and butt, dropping my Daisy. I was caught red-handed—on his
property with a gun, about to kill one of his pets—
and yet he seemed to have a peaceful look on his
face. I was confused.

Then Mr. Riley extended his hand, holding out to
me the live multi-colored pigeon. "Look how beautiful," he said kindly.

I blinked rapidly, then focused on the bird as I
leaned back on my hands in the dirt.
I had never been so close to a live
pigeon. He was beautiful. He blinked
with an eyelid just like mine. I looked
back at Mr. Riley. He smiled.
I looked at the calm bird again. His
feathers looked as smooth as fur,
and his mouth moved as if trying
to talk, while his head quickly
darted about, analyzing the situation. I relaxed a bit but remained
puzzled.

Mr. Riley said, "Here, you take
him," extending his finger toward

me. I looked at Mr. Riley then back to the bird. Sitting up, I hesitantly extended my right index finger, touching the end of Mr. Riley's finger. The bird trustingly hopped onto my finger. He was heavy and his feet were strong and warm. Mr. Riley stroked the bird's head, continuing down his back, nodding for me to do likewise. I did. The bird blinked. I was fascinated as the bird began to slowly open and close his mouth.

"Feel his chest," Mr. Riley encouraged. I curled my left hand slowly and gently around his warm chest. The bird was still. Then I felt the beating of his heart.

I looked to Mr. Riley and said with concern, "His heart is beating really fast."

"That's normal. Birds' hearts beat fast."

I moved my fingers to the bird's legs and feet. They were rough. Then the bird hopped to Mr. Riley's hand and up to his shoulder, peering at me as he continued to move his head in small jerks. Mr. Riley stood up from his kneeling position and extended his right hand to help me stand. I accepted. Mr. Riley moved toward me, and I took a step back as he lifted my BB gun from the weeds. He handed the gun to me. I was more confused.

"I got to get back to the store," he stated simply. Then he turned and walked into the orchard toward his house with the pigeon perched on his shoulder. He stopped, looked back at me, and said, "Come visit me and my birds sometime." He turned and disappeared through the trees.

I stood next to the fence, gun in hand, and realized I didn't know Mr. Riley at all.

Superman

*"I loved those nights when I would
fall asleep and dream I was flying."*

I loved those nights when I would fall asleep and
dream I was flying. I would run as fast as I could and
jump into the air, my arms stretched out to the side,
and begin to float. I would struggle for more altitude
until I rose to the top of the house and finally above
the telephone poles and trees, completely weightless,
and able to turn with a gentle twist of my body.

Ben and I finished watching *Superman* one morning on TV and decided flying didn't look that difficult after all. The only apparent difference between
Superman and us seemed to be the cape. So we
grabbed two large towels and headed for the garage
roof.

We stood in the shade next to the wood-clad sin-
gle-car garage with its sagging double doors. The
twin tree trunks that grew beside the garage were
perfectly spaced for the used boards we nailed to the
trunks, making a ladder to our rooftop perch.

Ben was three years older than I, a head taller, and possessed a sense of adventure that would make Lewis and Clark proud. Standing next to the garage, we surveyed the building height and measured our courage. The roof was more than twice as tall as we were. We felt the ground. It was harder than we had remembered.

"Do you think it'll work?" I asked Ben.

"It worked for Clark Kent, so I don't know why it won't work for us," Ben said, peering through his Coke bottle lenses.

I swallowed. "What if it doesn't?"

Ben, being smarter, replied, "We don't weigh as much as Superman. Everything should work perfect." The "should" really bothered me.

Ben began to climb the ladder. I followed. The roof seemed taller than before. We both stepped onto the black-shingled roof and sat, allowing our courage to gather. Ben stuck his finger in his mouth, then checked the wind direction. His father was in the Air Force, so he knew about these things.

"It seems we should jump south into the breeze," Ben calculated.

I calculated that he meant I should jump into the breeze. I walked to the south end of the hip-roofed garage and looked down. Failure looked somewhere between painful and lethal. I walked to the west side of the garage and looked down on our huge sandbox below. I felt only slightly better.

"Well, let's get our capes on and fly!" Ben encouraged. He tied the ends in a knot around my neck and I did the same for him. We each checked the double knots with hand tugs. They wouldn't come off. But the big question was whether they would hold enough air to allow us to fly—or was Superman's cape magic?

Ben didn't seem worried. I deduced that he had a plan, and the plan was me. I could see the headlines in the *Hollis County Weekly*: "8-YEAR-OLD AND 11-YEAR-OLD KILLED IN ROOFTOP FALL."

"Ben, you're older and you should go first," I tried.

Retreating, Ben replied, "This was your idea and you are going first. Besides, you're lighter."

"Then let's jump together," I suggested.

"You're lighter, and if you hit the ground you won't land as hard. It probably wouldn't even hurt."

I wasn't buying the lighter, younger, dumber approach. I was feeling queasy, and the fumes rising from the black roof weren't helping. "I'll go if you go," I finally said.

Ben walked all around the roof with more seriousness, finally deciding on the softer sandbox side rather than his finger-in-the-wind analysis. "Okay, let's do it," he said, swallowing hard. "Superman jumps in the air with his arms up, so that's how we should do it," he added.

I looked at Ben with a sense of finality as he took off his glasses and placed them on the ridge of the roof. We stood side by side. "Now, it's all in the aerodynamics of the goddamn cape," Ben added confidently. I loved it when Ben talked airplane language that he had picked up in the military, especially when he added expletives.

We shuffled to the edge of the roof. "Let's go on the count of three," Ben suggested. We looked below with fear of death. We looked above with dreams of flight. We calculated that it was worth the risk. Ben counted with increasing volume and fear in each number. "One . . . Two . . . Three . . . Go-o-o-o," and we both jumped up and out from the edge of the roof with arms extended heavenward. We  flew up about a foot then down about eight with duet screams of, "Ohhhhhhh," landing on our feet and burying past our ankles in the sand before the rest of our bodies slammed to the ground.

Dazed, Ben asked, "You okay, kid?"

"Yeah, I think so," I said, rubbing my legs.

"Boy, that didn't much work," Ben painfully stated.

"Naw, that wasn't much fun," I added, trying not to cry. "I wonder what we did wrong?"

"Jump," Ben added soberly.

Mama

*"Mama could handle a hammer like a man—
and, if need be, a man like a hammer."*

Mama decided that I needed a playhouse and that she and I would build it. Mama—that's what I called my grandmother—was quite a woman. She stood 4'11", an inch taller than my grandfather. She could handle a hammer like a man—and, if need be, a man like a hammer. She hated laziness, whiskey, playing cards in the house, a book on top of the Bible, and anyone who didn't treat her grandchildren right. She loved gardening, climbing trees, chickens, her milk cow Bessie, churned butter, scratch biscuits, and ribbon cane syrup. She loved dogs and wept at their passing.

Mama was born in 1897 in the Willowville community on the outskirts of Turnip. She was the middle child of nineteen, raised on a farm, could read and write, but never drove a car. She grew up privileged in a farming sort of way because her father found a stash of Confederate gold on Lost Hill. At age seventeen, she married Papa, who was ten years older. She married a happy but poor man. Papa couldn't read or write, but he loved to sing and dance and tell tall tales, especially to his grandson. Papa retired as janitor of the Hollis County Courthouse, a job that he considered lucky to have, compared to his days of picking cotton from "can 'til can't" for a nickel a day.

Mama was fifty-one years older than I, but we were best buddies. She and Papa were my babysitters because Mother had returned to teaching school. Married life had been happy for Mama but afforded no frills. She never owned a house (my mother had bought theirs for them), drove nothing other than a team of mules and a hard bargain, and never ate in a restaurant or slept in a hotel. She made the clothes her six children wore, ate what she raised, prayed over supper, and spent all her extra time entertaining me.

We started building the playhouse one cool Monday morning in November after the morning sun dried the dew and before the Texas heat began to simmer. Mama's fenced patch of land measured two acres with a tiny white house near the road, and an orchard to the side containing peach, plum, apple, pear, and pecan trees, all planted by Mama. Behind her house, Turnip's most beautiful vegetable garden flourished in the rich rows of sandy loam that Papa tilled with a mule and a singletree yoke twice a year. Beyond the garden stood a two-hole outhouse that backed up to the cow lot and a low-roofed barn that Mama had built for her chickens and Bessie. The lot for chickens, cows, and an occasional calf was a pasture almost an acre in size, with rich dirt for digging fishing worms.

Mama had sent Papa on the one-mile walk to town this morning to buy a few assorted items, encouraging him to take his time and visit with his old friends inside and outside the courthouse. This was Mama's way of getting Papa out from under foot. She loved him, but his lack of skills and initiative was a source of irritation for her.

"Cody, can you carry these boards?" she asked me as she carefully pulled the used lumber from the tin-covered pile of wood she had saved for whatever needed repairing or building. She made sure that my boards were small and contained no rusty nails or scorpions.

"Yes, ma'am," I answered, eager to help.

Mama was dressed in a homemade full-length flour sack dress with a two-pocket apron and a bonnet tied under her chin. She wore brown cotton gloves, galoshes for snake protection, and, as always, a smile. She climbed trees like a ten-year-old, and it was her habit to run from place to place, just for the fun of it. She laughed at every opportunity, exposing a beautiful set of teeth that at night rested on her nightstand in a glass of water. If Mama hit her finger with the hammer, it was time to keep quiet because she would spit and mumble in a harsh tone turned the other direction.

Mama and I carried the load of lumber to begin the playhouse. The design was in her head and a milk bucket full of used nails at her side. She picked a shady spot for the playhouse, one that enjoyed the southeasterly breezes of "Hooker's Hill," and she began marking and sawing the thick boards for the floor. She had only one hammer that she had soaked in a water bucket all night to tighten the head and a short handsaw that Papa kept razor sharp for her. She hammered and sawed as Tinker and Bobby, Mama's "fine dogs," and I watched in amazement.

Unencumbered by precision, Mama pretty soon had a floor built that was probably 6' x 6' and she was ready for the walls. We made more trips to the woodpile for lumber, careful not to step on a nail and get lockjaw. I never knew how lockjaw worked, but it sounded horrible.

By mid-morning, we were tuckered out and decided to sit a spell. The dogs lay in the shade, where they had dug shallow holes to soak up the cool. I sat in my ladder-back watching chair with rope bottom, while Mama sat on the playhouse floor with her shoes off, rubbing the dogs with her feet and borrowing some cool from the dirt.

I fetched a fresh bucket of cool water from the well, only recently having been entrusted with well privileges. As I extended the first dipperful to Mama, she insisted, "No, Cody, you first." I drank like I'd put in a full day's work, pitching the excess water toward the fence. Dipping Mama a fresh drink, I handed it over as she smiled at my kindness and drank heartily, water dripping from her chin. "I'll have one more," she said. I gave her another dipperful, which she almost finished, pitching the extra on her nearest plant.

"Do you like building things, Cody?" she asked genuinely, her blue eyes looking directly at me through gold-rimmed glasses.

"Yes, ma'am, I sure do!" I replied energetically. "And I'm learning a lot." Mama had been letting me finish sawing the boards that she had almost completed, and she let me hammer the nails that were mostly finished. We were a great team.

There was no sign of Papa and, other than the dogs perking up for an occasional passing car or a taunting bird landing nearby, all was quiet. We worked until we heard the downtown fire siren announce noon. I was amazed that we could hear such a small device from a mile away. Mama lay down the hammer on the floor of my new house, and I placed the saw beside it. We headed to the wash pan on the back porch, only to see Papa's smiling face as he opened the rickety gate to the back yard and looked toward the playhouse.

"Looks like a good start," Papa offered, obviously impressed but not surprised.

"Cody did most of the work," Mama said, trying to sound sincere.

"That right, Cody?" Papa asked.

"Well, not exactly," I replied shyly, looking up at Mama.

Papa patted me on the back as we walked up the sagging wooden steps to the tiny back porch, whose inside resembled the pickup bed of a truck farmer on Saturday morning.

We washed up, helping each other as we poured

water from the bucket into the pan, throwing out the dirty remains when we had finished.

Papa and I sat at the round oak table in the kitchen, removing the dishtowel which covered the homemade biscuits and hotcakes left over from breakfast. Mama retrieved the extra sausages from the stovetop and opened a new jar of dewberry jelly from her canning closet. Out of the Frigidaire came a bowl of churned butter. Then she sat down to join us. She removed another cloth from a plate revealing teacakes, which brought a smile from Papa and me. We enjoyed lunch and laughed as Papa regaled us with stories of his downtown adventure, with Mama often trying to simmer down his extravagances with a chiding, "Now, Hooker . . ." Hooker was my grandfather's nickname, earned while riding a horse bareback into town at a full gallop, interspersed with sudden stops to rear the horse as the downtowners encouraged, "Hook her." I, too, joined in with the energetic telling of playhouse building, taking more credit than I deserved—with not so much as a raised eyebrow from Mama.

Mama cleared the table as Papa and I finished every crumb of the teacakes. When all the dishes were in the dishpan, Papa rubbed his pooched stomach, popped his suspenders, and headed for his chair beside the Philco. As the tubes warmed and Papa dialed in the farm report, Mama and I readied ourselves for an afternoon's work on our project. The dogs wagged and panted at the banging of the screen door as they arrived with dirty noses from their excavations under the house.

We worked all afternoon and the remainder of the

week with essentially the same routine each day. Papa's only contribution was inspecting and praising our work, occasionally bringing us a board or a sack of shiny new nails from Hill's Lumber Hardware and Undertaking. Mama curiously ran out of nails almost every day.

Late Friday morning, Mama proclaimed the playhouse finished as she attached the spring to the screen door.

"Well, Cody, that ought to do it."

"Yes, ma'am," I replied, echoing Mama. "That ought to do it."

I opened the screen and went inside, inviting Tinker and Bobby and, of course, Mama.

"It's perfect!" I exclaimed, looking up at Mama. She beamed.

"It's all yours," she said, pulling my head to her apron.

Mama had built two beds just my size, covered with old quilts, as well as a table and two chairs that were also just my size. There were windows with screens and a tarp that rolled down to cover the opening in cold or rainy weather. She had also built shelves for dishes, spoons, spools, empty cans, and toys. The floor was covered with linoleum that she had rolled up and stored underneath her house. The playhouse had two doors, one screen and one solid and both with latches.

Sitting on one of the little beds, she asked, "Is this about what you had in mind?"

"Oh, no, ma'am, it's so much better than I imagined. It's like a real house! I love it. We did a great job!"

I smooched for the dogs to join me on my quilted bed, and they obliged, rewarding me with wet kisses. The four of us filled the playhouse like two families in a storm cellar. I stretched out on my bed and placed my head in the perfectly located window that looked toward the gate and the highway. Mama reached over and stroked Tinker's head, causing her tail to wag. We now had a place to play and make mud pies with assistance from the dogs and no rules. I would entertain myself there for years to come.

Mama took off her shoes, gloves, and bonnet, and rubbed her brow upward, brushing back her thick, curly brown hair which sprang right back in place. I marveled at her being almost sixty with not a single gray hair.

She sat beside me on my bed, shooing the dogs to the floor, and said, "Roll over, Cody." I rolled to my stomach, and she began scratching my back as I lay in the window with the sweet fragrances of her garden seeping through my screened window and filling the playhouse. A gentle breeze blew across me as Mama hummed and the birds serenaded. The world was perfect, as was my playhouse . . . and Mama.

Chili

"Come on in, boy, and close the door before all the meat ruins. That old door opens real easy . . . most times."

I had never stopped to think about the origin of meat that accompanied almost every meal at our house until the day I stood before Chili McMillan, the butcher at the Turnip Locker Plant.

It was hot, but summer was not yet in its prime. School was out for three whole months. I had just finished the fourth grade, but education was not taking a holiday. I entered the locker plant through the back screen door adjacent to the tall wooden fence that squeezed cattle into a standing-room-only pen where mud, urine, and manure squished up between their hooves. Pigs were cordoned off from cattle with plenty of wallowing

space. The stink was so strong I could taste it as it
drifted through Chili's screen door, accompanied by
grunting, squealing, bellowing animals that seemed
to sense their fate.

The Turnip Locker Plant was a thriving business
located in a building that was about half the size of
my school's gymnasium. The locker was a combination small grocery store and meat market in front,
with Chili's butcher shop in the back. As the only
meat-processing facility in this agriculturally based
community, the business enjoyed a corner on the
market.

Chili had invited me to watch him carve steaks
the last time I was in the locker plant shopping for
meat with my mother. He made sure his invitation
did not reach her ears. My interest in watching Chili
butcher originated with more curiosity about Chili
than his work.

As the rickety screen door slammed behind me
and my bare white feet absorbed the coolness from
the concrete floor, there stood the marvel of a man.
Adorned in black rubber boots and what had been a
white butcher jacket, topped-off with a too-small,
brown, short-brimmed felt hat turned up on all
sides, was Chili McMillan.

When the door slammed, Chili turned with carving knife in hand to see who approached his terri-
tory. Sensing alarm I squeaked, "Hello, Chili," which
brought an easy ear-to-ear grin from the huge black
man, dispelling apprehension on both sides. Chili's
teeth flashed of ivory and gold, and a deep and natural laugh rose up from his strong torso.

"How you doin', boy?" Chili greeted as he

slipped his knife into the sheath over his right hip pocket.

"Just fine, Chili. I came by to see if I could help."

Another deep and easy laugh followed as Chili's eyes glistened like that of an inspired teacher. Standing erect and placing both huge fists on his hips, Chili asked rhetorically, "Ever butcher a beef, boy?"

Swallowing heavily at the graphic thought, I managed a "No, sir," my eyes falling to Chili's rubber boots.

"Didn't think so," came the reply, as Chili turned back to the carcass hanging on the meat hook suspended from the ceiling. As the deliberate hand movements of his artistry began, he asked in a genuine tone, "Wanna learn?"

I looked toward his face, which was focused on his task, and replied, "Yes, sir, Chili. I sure wish you would teach me," not realizing what actions my mouth had just committed me to.

Another belly laugh, and the carving strokes continued without conversation.

Chili was a man rightly proud of his skill and pleased with the prospect of a student to break the monotony of his day. He also realized that a boy of ten was fascinated with life and death, curious about the event of dying, and interested in blood and guts and body parts.

Body parts were actually what attracted me to the locker plant that day. Not animal body parts, but Chili's body parts. The thought of an up-close look at Chili or, even better, a handshake was more temptation than I could resist. Chili was a strong, heavy-set man with skin the color of a Hershey bar and an age that I couldn't begin to guess. I assumed he was about the age of my father because they had played sandlot baseball together with mutual respect for each other's ability. Chili had a round face that matched his stomach. His eyes were clear and bright with a mischievous glint when just he and I were together. But when white cattlemen brought in their beef and talked down to Chili, his head would dip, his eyes would dull, and I could feel his hatred as he limited his acknowledgments to "Yassur." He understood whites. He didn't like a lot of them. He knew what they were capable of. But Chili, like all the other black folks in Turnip in 1958, didn't cause trouble. He needed his job and had to make the best of it. There were no alternatives.

I had heard that Chili had something that no other black man and no other white man had. I had never been allowed a penetrating view of Chili, so I relished the thought of quenching my curiosity. As I watched Chili carve, I moved closer to gaze at his mammoth appendages. Chili was big all over. If my dad weighed 200 pounds, Chili must have weighed three. His thick neck mirrored that of the wrinkled bulls he so gently sculpted. His head was in proportion to his neck with a flat nose the size of my fist and nostrils that looked like they could hold Vienna sausages. His chest and arms so completely filled his shirt that even the slightest movement revealed the massive structure beneath.

As Chili steadied the hanging carcass with his left hand and carved with his right, I got a prolonged view of what I had come to see. Hands. There they were: thick, solid, and strong. As he gripped his knife, my eyes froze on his fingers and I began counting at the thumb. One, two, three, four, five—and there it was. Six. He really did have six fingers! I glanced at the other hand, and there it was again. Six fingers on each hand.

As I studied the sixth finger, it wasn't what I had expected. It didn't grow out of his hand; it grew out of his little finger, which was anything but little. The sixth finger was tiny and fat, only about one-third the size of his little finger. It even had a nail. It was short and pudgy and looked out of place on such a large and perfect specimen, but there it was, attached by a piece of flesh smaller in diameter than a pencil lead.

I watched Chili carve for quite some time, not bothering him and only occasionally glancing at his eyes to see if my gawking was a problem. His baby finger didn't get in his way, and he never came close to cutting it off.

After a while I was satisfied. I had seen what I had come to see and I understood that questions would have to await a relationship.

But my education was not to end just yet. I had momentarily forgotten my commitment to help Chili. As he finished the carcass, which didn't at all resemble a cow, he eased underneath and lifted it off the hook effortlessly, using only his legs. As he began moving toward the large latched cooler door, Chili asked kindly, "Can you get the door, boy?"

"You bet!" came my automatic reply as I hurried in front of what was enough weight to squash me dead three times.

I grasped the cold, heavy, cast-iron cooler latch with both hands and saw the grisly evidence of Chili's profession all around the latch. As I strained, pulling the thick door open, a cool white cloud fell on my bare feet. I moved aside as Chili stepped over the threshold. Then he beckoned with a flick of his head, "Come on in," in a tone reminiscent of my schoolmates chiding "chicken." I swallowed and hesitated.

Peeking inside I saw, suspended from the frigid ceiling, a single light bulb which looked as if it could burn out at any moment. The room was about half the size of my schoolroom. As I stood on the warm side of the threshold with the ice cold latch in my hands and a cold cloud moving across my feet, I quickly inspected the thick door to see if the latch was operable from the inside. I was uncertain. I quickly glanced at all four walls of the dimly lit room full of hanging carcasses and saw no other exit. My pulse quickened and my breathing became rapid and shallow as I considered leaving. I didn't want Chili to see my fear, but I estimated it would take no more than ten minutes to either run out of oxygen or, more likely, freeze to death.

I didn't really know Chili, but Chili read my thoughts and apparently couldn't resist testing my courage and trust. "Come on in, boy, and close the door before all the meat ruins. That old door opens

real easy . . . most times." I suddenly hated my curiosity. I felt trapped. I didn't like it, but I knew I
had to go in or I would never find out if he also had
six toes and if his little finger really did work. My
eyelids batted back my skepticism. I inhaled as
deeply as I could and lifted my hesitant foot over the
threshold. As my second leg followed, I released the
spring-loaded door and it clamped shut behind me. I
held my breath as my bare feet began to stick to the
frozen concrete floor. I rotated onto the balls of my
feet as Chili hung the beef on the ceiling-mounted
hook with more care and time than was necessary.

Chili stood boldly with his hands propped on his
hips and said in an intimidating deep tone, "You
scared, boy?"

My heart missed several beats and my stomach
rose to my throat as I contemplated this mammoth
black man holding my life in the balance. I uttered,
"Yes, sir, I guess I am," knowing all too well that no
one could hear my screams for help from inside the
thick concrete walls with the cooler running. Chili
broke into a fit of laughter, finally folding double,
and slapping his huge hands together. Slowly regaining his composure, he looked up, winked, and said,
"Well, then, let's get the hell outta here!"

Relief engulfed me as I sprang to the door. To my
delight the latch lifted and I put my shoulder to the
door. As I pushed it open, the warm, heavy air hit
my face and I saw streaks of sunlight from the upper
windows of the butcher room. It looked like heaven.
Instantly, my insides began to resurrect themselves.

Chili continued laughing. With his hand gently
patting my shoulder he said, "Come with me, boy,

I'm gonna make a butcher out of you." I had the uneasy feeling that I had not jumped the last hurdle on
this obstacle course.

Feeling began returning to my cold feet as I
walked out into the butcher shop. The concrete floor
had a slippery Crisco texture and sloped to a single
iron grate in the center of the room. The walls were
pale green tile block. Among the few accessories in
the room were a short white bench for Chili, a heavy-
legged butcher block table with knives, a sharpener,
and a hack saw hanging on the side, and an ancient,
blood-stained single-shot .22 rifle standing in the
corner. The room had good natural light, and a ceiling fan stirred the only breeze in the room.
Opportunities for Chili to be distracted or to take a
rest were nil.

Chili whistled as he readied the room for his next
task and my education. He washed his hands at the
deep wall-hung sink and walked over to lift the rifle
from the corner. "You ready?" he asked in honesty.

"Yes, sir," I replied, unable to disguise my apprehension.

"Then go pick me out a beef and run him through
the chute."

I exited the screen door to where the miserable
cattle were standing in the muck of their pen. I
looked at the cattle, whose eyes held no hope—or
so it seemed to me. I'd shot birds and squirrels
and snakes but never a large animal and never a
tame one. I suddenly wished to be anywhere else in
the world, even in the cooler. My attention was bro-
ken by Chili's hollering from inside: "Come on, boy,
we ain't got all day. I got to skin all them beefs

before dark." I hated myself and my curiosity concerning Chili's abnormality. Now I felt like the abnormality.

I opened the chute, and fortunately the cattle did their own selecting as the first innocent steer anxiously opted for the illusion of escape. "Slam that gate and be quick about it," Chili resounded in a business tone. "I don't want but one at a time." I obeyed as the steer stutter-stepped to the end of the chute, with Chili sliding a board behind his flank so he couldn't back out.

The steer realized his options had ended as he uneasily faced Chili. He pushed and twisted against the wooden rails of the chute with violent jerks of his head as I backed away, retreating behind Chili.

Chili reached under his butcher apron into his khaki pants pocket and placed one small single shell in the chamber of the .22 rifle. The bolt-action rifle had a ring of finality to it as Chili slapped it shut with his right hand. He glanced to see that I was clear, then hoisted the rifle to his shoulder and whistled a piercing whistle. The steer stopped to devote his entire attention to Chili. With enough experience to require no aim, Chili fired the tiny slug directly into the steer's brain. Blood spurted from the straw-sized hole between the steer's eyes. The animal fell to his knees and then fully to the floor, with only one deep groan announcing the exit of life. His mouth was open, with his tongue protruding onto the concrete floor, and his eyes stayed open, too, but life was leaving them. I wanted to vomit.

Chili turned to replace the rifle in the corner and picked up a curved bladed knife on his way toward the fallen steer. He opened the front gate of the chute, allowing the mammal to expand out into the room.

Chili's first move was to place the knife to the steer's throat. With one flick of his huge wrist the jugular vein was severed, and a huge stream of warm blood began to pump out of the steer with the rhythm of the last beats of his heart. The surging blood flowed toward the floor drain. The gushing flow diminished to a stream and then to a trickle as it coursed its way along the grisly concrete floor. I was amazed at the quantity of blood, which flowed for several minutes.

Chili then split the steer from throat to belly and up to his tail, allowing all the bowels and organs to spill out on the floor, careful not to puncture any parts. He then dissected the innards, using almost everything—heart, liver, kidneys. He placed these parts on the butcher block and put the throwaway guts over in a corner, which already had a pile from the day's earlier guests.

While I stood trying to absorb the sequence of events, Chili had gotten the water hose and turned on the faucet to begin washing the blood from the floor. He then tossed the end of the hose into the puddle of blood and began to wrap the rear feet of the steer together with a chain. After several wraps Chili slid the overhead pulley above the hindquarter of the steer and attached the pulley hook to the chained legs.

Not a word had been spoken. My mind was racing. My conscience was calculating. Finally, Chili said, "Okay, boy, now pull on this chain and raise him up." I couldn't imagine being able to hoist this huge animal into the air, but I did as Chili said. The pulley began to clatter as the chain passed through it. I was as amazed at being able to hoist the steer as I was that so tiny a bullet could kill so strong a beast in mere seconds.

As the animal was raised, the flow of blood returned. I pulled. The chain clattered. And the blood flowed. "That's high enough," Chili announced. The steer's feet were as high as a basketball goal and his blood-drenched tongue was scarcely off the floor.

Chili walked to the rutted butcher-block table, lifted his carving knife, and began to slide it rhythmically back and forth across a hand-held sharpener. The sound of steel against steel reverberated from the walls. Goosebumps rose on my pale arms. After twenty or so quick motions, the blade glistened.

Beads of sweat trickled down Chili's face as he laid his knife on the table and stooped to pick up the water hose from the pool of blood. The water had continued to run throughout the process, washing the remains of blood down the drain. Chili lifted the hose from the blood, raised the end of it to his lips, and gulped water. Blood was on the floor. Blood was on Chili's hands and clothing. And blood was on the hose. After Chili had drunk his fill, he turned to me from his crouched position and with a challenging smile asked, "Want a drink, boy?" I shook my head in the only direction it could ever have moved, declining Chili's offer. He began to laugh again. I thought of the stories I had heard about Chili drinking warm blood from his kills, but I could not bring myself to ask.

Stepping over to the steer, he began the procedure he had done a thousand times before. There were no hesitations in his movements. He cut the cowhide around the steer's leg where it joined the body, then slit the hide down to the hoof and peeled it away. After four legs were done, the steer looked like he had on a sleeveless shirt. Chili then split the steer's hide into quadrants and peeled away all the skin. It sounded like removing adhesive tape from a baseball bat.

He then hacksawed off the hoofs and placed them in a box under the butcher block. Chili skinned the tail and sawed it off. The bones cut pretty much like small tree limbs. Chili then cut the steer's neck down to the spine and hacksawed the spine, allowing the head with its glazed eyeballs to roll onto the floor. The eyes and ears he didn't keep but the brain and tongue he did: he carefully ran his hand into the head from the neck and pulled out what looked like a heap of pale-colored noodles melted together. As he placed them in a pan, they spread out on the bottom. They looked anything but intelligent.

I was relieved to see that Chili didn't use the steer's penis. I had heard Vienna sausages were actually made from the penises of cattle and didn't want to see if that was true. I had eaten too many sausages to think about that possibility.

Chili finished up the steer and we placed him in the cooler. The latch felt reliable this time, and I wasn't worried. We repeated the process twice more before Chili said, "Okay, boy, I'll go get the next beef and you can shoot him. Ever shot a steer, boy?"

Suddenly, I found my voice and got rather talkative. "Well, only one, Chili, and I only shot him in the balls with my BB gun. It didn't kill him, but it sure made him mad when it thudded against his drooping bag of balls. He let out a mean groan and threw dirt around a while and kept hitting himself with his tail. He was behind a fence, too, and I've only shot a .22 a few times when my uncle Ray took me squirrel hunting. My dad doesn't hold much with guns."

"Well, we'll be careful, and we won't have to tell your dad. I'll go get the steer, and you get the gun."

As I lifted the relic from the corner, it had a greasy feel to it. It didn't look deadly—it only had a small hole in the end of the barrel. But I had seen it work, and it certainly did the job.

Again I was forced to think about my position. I had come to get a glimpse of Chili's fingers and now found myself knee deep in what felt like murder. I was about to shoot a gun Daddy would violently disapprove of, and I was going to take a life—a big, innocent life.

Chili got the steer penned and walked toward me, reaching into his pocket for a bullet. I took the bullet from his huge palm and placed it into the chamber, which I had already opened. I carefully closed it, not wanting the bullet to explode, and was ready to shoot.

Chili looked me in the eye and asked, "Are ya ready, boy?"

"I guess so," came my hesitant reply.

"When I whistle, you take dead aim and shoot. Ready?"

"Yes, sir."

Then came the piercing whistle and a sudden stillness. I took aim, closed my eyes, and fired.

The steer let out a piercing screech of pain, and Chili grabbed the gun and began to cuss and reload. "Goddamn, boy! You shot him in the nose. Now I ain't ever gonna get him still. Goddamn son-of-a-bitch."

Chili reloaded and walked toward the steer, whose head was jerking wildly while his body banged against the wooden chute. Placing the gun next to the steer's ear, Chili fired a bullet into his brain, dropping the steer just like all the others.

Chili wasn't happy. We didn't talk much until the steer was lifted in the air. Then, in an act of consolation, Chili asked if I wanted to split him open. I needed to regain some respect so I recited, "Yes, sir," even though I knew by now I didn't have the stomach for butchering.

As I inserted the knife into the neck slit and began to open the steer, I was surprised at the strength required to cut the cowhide. Soon my right hand couldn't do the job alone and I had to lend my left. As I got down to the stomach, Chili said, "Now be careful"—and just about the same time, the knife sunk all the way in and ruptured the intestine. I looked up at Chili and his black face was turning red. He cussed quietly this time and to himself as he took the knife from my hand and continued cutting the steer. The stench was unbearable, but I stayed beside Chili. I only hoped I wouldn't vomit on Chili as I looked over his shoulder. He pulled the insides over to the heap in the corner, and I became more accustomed to the odor. Chili talked less during the next hour and simply did his chores. I was relieved that there was only one more steer to slaughter. As Chili was finishing the final carving, his tension eased and we laughed and talked.

"Chili, do you like butchering?" He looked at me and could read my distaste for the art.

"Yeah, I reckon I do, boy. It's all I know. That and barbecuing. I been butchering since I wasn't much older 'n you. Yeah, I reckon I like it all right. How you like it, boy?"

We both smiled and I said, "I don't know if I'd be much good at it. I'm thinking about going to college and being a schoolteacher."

Chili looked down and said, "That'd be real nice. Teachin' is good work."

We visited a little more, then Chili went over to the little white bench, sat down, and began to pull off his rubber boots. I was all eyes. Chili sat his white-socked foot down on the slab and began pulling his other boot off. His foot was wide enough for six toes, and I asked without thinking.

"Chili, do you have six toes, too?" I felt embarrassed as the words spilled from my mouth. Chili was caught off guard by my directness but recovered quickly.

"Shore do, boy. Just like on my hands," as he raised his right hand and opened the palm to scrutinize his own features. He bent down and pulled off his sock and let me see. "Ever see anything like that, boy?"

"No, sir, I sure haven't, Chili. It looks real good. Do they work?"

Chili began to laugh at me and gently pound me on the back with his open palm. "Naw, boy, they don't much work, but they shore do get in the way." As he slipped his sock back on and placed his foot into his shoe, the problem was evident. "See how I had to cut a hole in the side so my little toe can breathe?"

"Yes, sir. Sure looks risky, Chili. You could knock that thing off if you weren't real careful."

Chili laughed again. "Guess so, boy. Guess so."

As Chili readied to leave, I said, "Well, Chili, I got to be going home. Mother's gonna wonder where I'm at."

"'Preciate the help, boy. Now what's yore firs' name," which was Chili's only act of uncertainty during the day.

"Cody . . . Cody Walker," I announced.

"Well, Cody, thanks for the help. You come back to see me now, you hear?"

"Yes, sir, Chili, I sure will. Thanks for letting me come down."

"And you come out to Rose Hill some Sunday when I'm barbecuing and try some o' my chicken. You'll like it."

"I will, Chili. Thanks." As the screen door slammed behind me, my burdened mind recounted the events of the last several hours. My emotions ran from excitement to curiosity to guilt to supremacy over animals and inferiority regarding Chili. Today I had certainly eliminated one career option, never to question the decision again. I had seen more blood and more fingers and toes than I would ever see again. I had made friends with a good man who cared for children. He also happened to be black, but that was of no concern to Chili and me. ✾

Bringing in the Sheaves

"Preachers rotated through Turnip fairly often. The good ones wouldn't stay—and the bad ones wouldn't go."

Church in Turnip was enough to scare the hell out of you. Heaven and hell were serious business. Heaven was the unattainable gleam in the preacher's eye. Hell was the red-faced glare the raised podium prophet thrashed us with thrice per week.

Turnip was a three-church town, consisting of Conservative, Ultra-Conservative, and Radically Conservative but identified as Methodist, Baptist, and Church of Christ. I was a Church of Christer, and not just a regular one—a serious three-time-a-weeker, which was the only way to tell the real Christians from the "fringers." Neither rain nor shine, Walt Disney nor the World Series interfered with church. Putting the Lord second was a ticket straight to hell, which meant summer revivals took precedence over even the love of my life—Little League baseball. Moreover, we were told to feel *good* about our sacrifice. It was my first encounter with masochism. My first encounter with eternity was revival week. I hated revivals, and from the looks on the congregation's and preachers' faces, they hated them, too.

Turnip was not merely in the Bible Belt, it was the buckle—the Antioch of Western Civilization. We had one book, the Bible, and not just any Bible—the King James version, which evidently had been christened by God himself. Other versions were thought to have been tampered with, but not the Holy King James version. It was the one with the "thees" and "thous" which we spoke and prayed with on Sundays and Wednesdays so God would understand us better.

At the Church of Christ we didn't have to worry about other interpretations of the Bible, for there was only one—the one *our* preacher had learned at preacher school and dictated to us. There was an uneasy comfort in knowing we were the only ones who were right. We had the truth, the whole truth, and nothing but the truth, and it was our duty to convert the whole world to Church of Christdom. We took a great deal of sadistic pride in our self-righteousness. There was one church and only one church—the Church of Christ—commonly referred to by its members as THE Church. It was pure and simple: if you didn't go to the Church of Christ, you went to hell. No questions asked.

The Church was an accepting church, much like Hitler's Third Reich. We were the chosen. Well, I've got to admit, the thought of all my friends going to hell was not much comfort to me. The miserable guilt I felt was compounded by the fact that it was

my duty to convert them to the Church or they
would burn forever.

We had to memorize all the verses that proved
that the Baptists and Methodists were going to hell
in order to convert them. So armed with a Church of
Christ pamphlet and fired-up with a guilt-laden hellfire and brimstone sermon, off I would go to visit my
friends and save the lost. Thus ensued heated argu-
ments on right and wrong. Then ultimately my duty:
to tell them they were going to hell.

I've got to tell you, our church didn't make many
friends.

Soon I began to look at who was going to heaven
and who was going to hell, and for the first time a
new question came to mind: which way did I want
to go? The Methodists, Baptists, and my friends
were all going to hell, not to mention some of my
close family. And who was going to heaven? Well,
the preacher for sure, and the elders, most of the
deacons and some of the Sunday school teachers. For
the rest of us the odds were pretty slim. It was calculated for us that only about five percent of the
church would make it, but I suppose it was the fire
that converted me. The thought of burning forever
pretty much frightened the hell out of me.

The formula for eternity in bliss was regularly
laid out in five steps accompanied by verse: hear,
believe, repent, confess, and be baptized. But that
was too easily accomplished for a ladder-climbing,
heaven-earning Church of Christer. So each Sunday
more criteria were added by our interpreter of
God's Book, the omnipotent preacher. They were, to
mention only a few: no pianos, communion every

Sunday, church three times a week, praying without ceasing, singing with the spirit and the understanding, baptism by immersion only, keeping the Ten Commandments, and not adding or subtracting anything from the King James version. Then, simply living a morally and spiritually perfect life, free of even thinking a sin because thinking a sin and committing a sin were the same thing—then and only then did you have a chance of heaven. Oh yes, and you couldn't be divorced or rich, because it was easier for a camel to go through the eye of a needle than for a rich man to go to heaven. A somewhat rigorous obstacle course, it seemed to me. We were a works church. We had nothing to do with that namby-pamby, saved-by-grace bit. No siree, we had the rules, and we planned to follow 'em and earn our way to heaven.

In our church we didn't speak in tongues or have healings, and we certainly didn't have "instruments of music." We spoke where the Bible spoke and were silent when the Bible was silent. I figured the Bible must have spoken a lot about hell because that's all we heard! That and bringing in the sheaves. The sheaves were lost sheep, the preacher said, and we were the flock. I thought of sheep as the ones who would follow the leader over the cliff, so it seemed an appropriate name to me.

We lived and "loved" God out of fear. My fear was actually directed more toward our many preachers. The expression on their faces was universal and frightening. It was anger and guilt and hatred and warning. They said it was love, but it sure didn't feel like love to me.

Sermons were rough. The rougher, the better, so the congregation said. "Beat on us, preacher, we like it," was the mood. Our congregation had a penchant for red-faced preachers who could "chop wood." Chopping wood was the lashing we needed so we would be good and bring in the sheaves. Sheaves were also the lost of the world, like the Africans. We were to bring them in, too, but be sure they weren't black. Black souls were to be handled by black Churches of Christ, supposedly.

Church of Christ preachers rotated through Turnip fairly often. The good ones wouldn't stay— and the bad ones wouldn't go. In between, we interviewed. It was difficult having to listen to so many illiterate preachers lash out with so much anger the dogma the Church had seared into their hearts. And, on top of that, my mother would make me pump their hand at the door on my way out and tell them in a believable tone how much I enjoyed their sermon.

During those years I saw more scowled faces, heard more screaming sermons, and felt more damned than Shadrach, Meshach, and Abednego. The only things that kept me going through those dark days were the preachers' daughters.

Two in particular come to mind—sisters. One my age, the other two years older. We were at or about puberty. I would sit next to one of them, and when we would have to stand and sing I had to keep my songbook front and center, just below my belt. Their bulges made me bulge, and their smiles acknowledged that they were familiar with lowered songbooks. They smiled as they sang. My heart was filled with a certain joy as well. It was then that my three-time-a-week vigils paid off, for I knew the songs by heart. It would be years before my songbook would move up.

So, there we would sit, the teenagers all to-gether—hard pews, hard sermons, and hard extrem-ities. A little bit of heaven in a sea of hell. These sis-ters were not what I envisioned a preacher's daughter to be. As a mat-ter of fact, they didn't fit any of the criteria other than attendance. I suppose that's what attracted me to them—that and their breasts, which would make a Jersey cow proud. My dream each Sunday was to just accidentally touch one of them. The thought of what that mass of firm flesh felt like was almost more than my songbook could bear. What memories. In actuality, I only got an occasional elbow feel. But I was satisfied. I was also relieved that they were the real thing and not a wad of Kleenex.

Yes, there were many thought-provoking hours spent in those hard times while looking innocently into their father's eyes with the apparent interest of a monk.

From the pulpit of that small rock church build-ing, with its hundred or so members, I heard ser-mons that would chill a snowman. We were told that drinking root beer was a sin, because it would lead to drinking beer, which was a big enough sin to send you straight to hell. If you missed a church service and you died or the end of the world came before you had a chance to make it up, you were a goner. If you didn't sing you were probably a goner. And if you were a young man and you didn't preach, you were at best doubtful on making the pearly gates.

One Sunday I remember coming in fifteen minutes late, and the preacher looked me straight in the eye and in the middle of his sermon said, "And some of you are only fifteen minutes from hell." Well, hell, I didn't figure I had a Chinaman's chance, so I simply gathered up a few of my own thoughts, primarily concerning the sisters, and persevered.

I envied my dad. He slept on Sundays. I knew he was going to hell, but he seemed to be enjoying the trip—which was more than I could say for our congregation. Mother and Daddy didn't talk religion much. If they did, it was tense. Mother was a hard-liner. Daddy was too, but in the opposite direction. He was an educated and intelligent man, a man of reason, who had mistakenly allowed himself to be lured into a revival at the Church. He didn't want any part of what he saw. He wasn't much on being told how to think, how to vote, and who was and was not going to heaven. So Sundays were newspaper and baseball game days for him, which made me yearn for adulthood and free choice.

Indelible in my memory are songs like "For Such a Worm as I" and "When That Awful Day We See" and the multiple invitation verses of "Oh, Why Not Tonight," with teary, pleading sermonettes between verses. But, yes indeed, we had the Bible, and the Bible was the "Good News," and the good news was "love," and the preacher said we were filled with it. The truth was, he was full of it—and I don't mean love.

So began the inner struggle of my life. That upbringing was a strong dose to take and proved to be a strong dose to overcome. 🐊

Bloody Bones
and Skinny Eyes

*"I heard Uncle Cliff throw the lever,
locking the door. Horror set in."*

Mysteriously I found myself on Uncle Cliff's
front porch. Uncle Cliff lived in a small, dilapidated
house with chickens under the porch and a crum-
bling picket fence to pen them in. His house was adjacent to the Turnip depot and across the railroad
tracks from the ice house. The railroad tracks were
one block from the courthouse square and two
blocks from my house and established my southern
boundary for adventure. Mother would only allow
me to cross the tracks to visit Uncle Cliff with special permission.

Uncle Cliff was my great uncle; he had no children. He had married my grandmother's sister. My
grandmother didn't have much use for Cliff Horton
and warned me to steer clear. I found him to be a

scary old man full of eerie tales.
He dressed in striped bib overalls
over a white shirt buttoned to
the collar which blended into his
pale skin and white hair. He
was frail-looking with dark
eyes recessed into circular
brown sockets which gave
him a ghostly appearance.
When he told stories about
"haints," his eyes grew
wild.

I had stolen over to
Uncle Cliff's for a visit. We were
sitting in rocking chairs side by
side on his front porch, watching
the butterflies and birds, not saying much, when we heard the
Old Katy train whistle in the
distance. As I looked at Uncle
Cliff, his eyes grew large and he tightened his grip
on the arms of the rocker, stopping the motion of
the chair. My senses heightened as I began to feel
the rumble of the massive steam locomotive making the last bend before the cotton gin and downtown. The whistle blew a cloud of smoke in the
air, and the brakes began to screech, making the
boxcars bang against each other as the Old Katy
slowed. We could see the conductor in his blue overalls with matching cap hanging out the engine
window as he measured his distance so the train
would stop perfectly in front of the elevated wooden
depot. When all the boxcars settled, a cloud of

steam hissed out of the wheels, announcing her arrival.

I turned to Uncle Cliff, who had not said a word since hearing the train. His body was tense. He lowered his chin, then quickly raised it to spit a wad of tobacco juice mostly over the porch railing as if to relieve his tension. He said seriously, "Well, Cody, you wanna go inside the house and lock the doors?"

I tensed. "Why, Uncle Cliff?"

Wiping his mouth with the back of his hand, which sounded like sandpaper as it crossed his white stubble, he said, "Well, Cody, there's haints in them boxcars." I swallowed and looked for more information. None came.

"What's a haint, Uncle Cliff?" I asked, not sure I wanted to know.

"Well, boy, a haint is a terrible thang. It lives in boxcars and it eats children," he explained as he turned and looked me dead in the eye. My fear intensified.

"Do you think there's any haints in those boxcars?" I pointed to the fifteen or twenty that now appeared to fence us in.

"I reckon they is. Only sometimes you can't see 'em." I was on my way inside when Uncle Cliff said, "You wanna go check it out?" I hesitated, not really wanting to go. I had never seen a haint, but I had heard my grandfather tell stories about them. My curiosity became stronger than my fear.

"Will they hurt us if we find them?"

"Well, they won't hurt me. They just take little children," Uncle Cliff replied as he slowly began to stand, pushing himself up on the arms of the tall rocking chair. "Let's go have a look-see." He shuffled his eighty-year-old body toward the porch steps, then turned, surprised to see me back in the rocker, "Ain't you comin', boy?"

Not moving, I countered, "Why don't we just look from here?"

"Well, boy, you ain't gonna see no haints from here. They hide in dark places durin' the daylight." He looked at me closer. "You scared, Cody?"

"No, sir," I said nervously. "I'm just not sure Mother would want me goin' around that train."

Uncle Cliff grinned slyly. "Well, then, we won't tell her." He turned and headed toward the train, motioning me with his hand. "Come on, boy! We'll be okay . . . unless we run into Bloody Bones and Skinny Eyes."

I was scared to go investigate, but I also didn't want to be left alone on the porch where some invisible haint could come and snatch me up, so I hopped out of the chair and walked in nervous jerks toward Uncle Cliff, grasping a wrinkled hand that wasn't offered and one that I had never held. Uncle Cliff looked down at me in surprise. "Okay then, boy." We walked cautiously until the boxcars were less than a stone's throw away.

"You pretty fast afoot, boy?"

I began to quiver as I thought to myself, *I'm a pretty fast runner for an eight-year-old, but how can I outrun something I can't see and something I don't know the size of?*

"How big's a haint, Uncle Cliff?"

He was stepping toward the open boxcar closest

to us. "Well, that's hard to say. Maybe ten feet tall, I guess. Some more, some less."

Ten feet tall! Something ten feet tall could snatch me up before I could get started.

I gripped the old man's hand harder as we neared the open car. I could smell the creosote ties and the oil from the train as I pondered my fate. The boxcar we were approaching was dark brown with writing on the side that was much more complex than my current reader featuring, "Run, Dick, run. Run. Run. Run." As we crossed the shallow ditch before reaching the gravel berm that elevated the tracks, my head was oscillating faster than a Westinghouse fan in August. I looked at Uncle Cliff, who seemed unconcerned with everything except his footing.

We made our way up the incline, slipping a bit on the large chunks of gray gravel. The boxcar doors were now within arm's reach of Uncle Cliff as I followed behind, keeping a death grip on his old hand. He looked down at me, then slowly stuck his head inside the boxcar. The floor was so high it almost reached his chin. He turned his head side to side taking a long look, then stopped to focus on the far right-hand corner. I looked up, but I was too short to see anything except the stained wooden undercarriage.

"Wanna look inside?"

My mind raced. My mouth wouldn't answer. Uncle Cliff made my decision as he reached down and lifted me from behind while boosting me up with his knee, until my chest was level with the boxcar floor. I put my hands on the plank floor as he held me. The metal door glide was hot and the wood floor was dirty and coarse. I hesitated, gathered my courage, then peeked inside. It was too dark to see the ends of the boxcar, but there were no signs of haints anywhere. My fear eased until I remembered that haints were sometimes invisible.

"Okay, Uncle Cliff, I've seen enough," I said, squirming to get down to the ground. Uncle Cliff tightened his grip under my arms, not letting me down.

I was confused.

Suddenly, with more strength then he should have had, Uncle Cliff pitched me into the boxcar and slammed the heavy metal door shut. I was in total darkness. Then I heard Uncle Cliff throw the lever, locking the door. Horror set in. I felt the rough timber floor against my hands and knees as I strained to see.

From the darkness, two closely cropped red eyes suddenly appeared high above the floor. I was terrified. I began desperately beating on the metal door, yelling, "Uncle Cliff, let me out! Let me out!" I was crying with fear as I heard Uncle Cliff's laughter grow more and more faint. He had left me. I pounded on the door, but there was no one to hear my cries.

I turned toward the two skinny eyes. They were now moving closer and closer and getting lower and lower. I could feel the hot breath of the creature. Suddenly, there was also a bloody skeleton moving toward me from the corner of the boxcar. I was coming out of my skin, and my heart was beating so fast I couldn't breathe. Then both haints lunged toward me with fierce hungry growls as I screamed for help. The instant before the savages grabbed me, I crashed to the floor, and heard Mother's pleasant voice.

"Cody, breakfast is ready."

Stand Your Ground

*"You boys go home and get your daddy and you tell him
to come down here because we're gonna fight!"*

It was an overcast summer's morning as my
brother Jim and I pedaled our Schwinn three-speed
bicycles around the narrow, paved streets near our
house and downtown Turnip. We were looking for
friends and adventure when we spotted the Jennings
brothers on their three horses, galloping toward us.
We turned at the next alley to avoid trouble, hoping
the brothers had not seen us. The Jennings brothers
were the town bullies. They were agreeable enough
individually, but when all three were together they
projected the sullen personality of their father.

Jim and I pedaled a couple more blocks before deciding to head for home. But as we slowed almost to
a stop in turning our bikes, out of nowhere came
Jake, Jack, and Wayne Jennings. They were high
above us on their horses. Our heads were no higher
than their knees. The horses were jumpy and moving
quickly side-to-side, trapping our escape just like the

cattle they worked. The horses did the talking for the intimidating threesome as their agenda of fear began to play itself out.

I was terrified, and I could see Jim was, too. One hoof could kill us as they forced the horses to rear up. I covered my head with my arms, attempting to duck while straddling my bike, as Jim pleaded, "What are you doing? You're gonna kill us! Get away! Get away from us!"

The youngest of the group, at age ten, I panicked and began crying, "You're gonna kill us. Please get away!" The boys laughed, spat tobacco at us, and jerked their horses into more of a frenzy.

Jim, three years my elder but considerably younger and smaller than two of the brothers, said strongly, "Get outta here! Get outta here!" trying to protect me and stand up to the trio. We maneuvered our bikes for daylight but found none.

Then Wayne, the oldest, looked at his older brothers and shouted, "Let's kill 'em!" in a serious tone, followed by, "What are you sissies gonna do now? Huh?" He kicked his horse in the flank and jerked the reins. Jim and I thought we were dead. The gang began to laugh as their spooked horses jumped all around us.

Jim, sensing we needed to do something quickly, turned to me and said, "Come on," as we jumped off our bikes and scampered up a nearby tree, leaving our bikes as a barricade the horses hesitated to cross.

From our perch the three circling horsemen began to goad, "You cowards. You want your mama? You're just a couple of cowards."

I thought to myself, *That sounds correct to me.*

The low limbs prevented the horses from getting close to us. We didn't know if the boys were going to pull us down and beat us up or have their horses do it for them.

Then Jack said to his brothers in disgust, "Come on, let's get outta here!" He taunted as they left, "We'll get you good next time!" Sinking their heels into the sweating horses, they galloped away.

I was trembling. My crying had stopped, but my thoughts continued racing. My fears did not subside. Jim looked spooked, too. We knew they could be lying in wait for us to come down from the tree or to round the next corner on our bikes. After some time passed, and with every nerve on red alert, we climbed down from the tree, quickly got on our bikes, checked all sides, and raced home.

Home never felt so good. We were safe near Mother, who was humming and cleaning the kitchen, oblivious to our brush with death.

We didn't leave the yard for the remainder of the day. At dinner that night, Daddy sensed a secret and inquired. Jim and I eyed each other, then Jim told him what had happened. Daddy, a large man of intimidating presence but few words, simply said, "We'll see about that tomorrow." Jim and I exchanged glances, not knowing what he meant.

The next morning arrived. It was Saturday, and yesterday seemed distant. After breakfast, Daddy asked Jim and me to join him for catch in the front yard. Daddy rarely played with us, so we jumped at the chance to toss the baseball.

The Jennings family lived two blocks from us in

a shabby house off the paved road. As fate would have it, the three brothers came strutting toward town, passing in front of our house. I wanted to hide. Jim was unsure what to do. Daddy was not. Burying the baseball hard in his brown leather glove, he walked to the edge of our yard abutting the one lane paved street and confronted the boys.

Red-faced and muscle-jawed, Daddy challenged directly, "You boys been scaring my boys?"

The Jennings brothers began veering to the other side of the street as Wayne said in a half snicker and swagger, "No, sir, we were just havin' a little fun. We didn't mean no harm."

Daddy, sounding madder, said, "You call rearing three horses up on two kids younger and smaller than you fun?"

Wayne sobered. "No, sir, I guess it wasn't much fun."

Daddy pressed further, moving toward the street. "You boys like to fight?" he said in earnest. I looked at Jim behind Daddy's back, astounded to hear what was coming out of my father's mouth.

"No, sir, we don't," Wayne replied immediately in an intimidated tone.

"I think you do." Daddy paused. "I like to fight, too," he said with conviction. Daddy looked through the three bullies and said, "I'll tell you what." I could hardly wait to hear the "what" as my adrenaline rushed. "You boys go home and get your daddy, and you tell him to come down here because we're gonna fight!"

I was incredulous! It would be four against three. The three brothers would kill Jim and me for sure, and I had never seen Daddy in action. In fact, this moment was the most action I had ever seen him in.

Wayne groveled. "No, sir, we don't want to fight. I'm sorry we scared your boys."

Daddy replied, "That dog won't hunt. You boys started this, and I'm going to finish it." Pause. "Are you gonna go get your daddy, or am I gonna have to?" I was visualizing a street brawl and sensed fear in the brothers.

"We don't want a fight, sir," Jack, the middle brother, added. "I'm sorry we scared your sons. It won't happen again."

"You boys like pushing little people around, don't you?" Daddy was not finished with them yet. No reply. "Why don't you go get your daddy and pick on someone your own size?" No reply. "You boys scared?" Pause. "You like being scared?" Pause.

Jake, the youngest brother, replied, "We don't want trouble, sir. We apologize. It won't happen again."

Daddy seemed to grit his teeth before he said, "If I hear of you boys, any of you," pointing his finger at each, "bullying my sons, I'm gonna come knocking on your door. You hear me?"

"Yes, sir," came the unanimous reply.

"You hear me?" he said again as if they were deaf.

"Yes, sir," each said again, dipping their heads. He stood glaring, then turned and walked toward the house. The trio slithered away, hunkered down as if shielding themselves from a rain of hot coals.

Daddy turned to Jim and me and said, "They won't be back. They're just like their daddy. They were looking for someone to run over and picked the wrong house." Exhaling deeply, he relaxed and placed a strong hand on each of our shoulders and said, "Don't back down from bullies. Stand your ground. If you don't stand it, nobody will." He paused, then added more gently, "Treat people right and help the little man." He began walking toward the front door.

Jim and I looked at each other and Daddy. I felt a bit taller.

Pulling open the screen door, he gave us a wry smile and said, "You boys could have taken care of your share, right?" With that he walked inside, closing the door.

Looking for Russians

*"We felt good about having protected the country
for one summer afternoon."*

Ben and I lay on our backs in the shade of a giant
pecan tree on the courthouse lawn. It was a lazy
summer's afternoon, and the smell of the fresh-cut
grass that cushioned our backs filled the air. Birds
were chirping in the hedges and trees, a few cars
moved slowly around the square, and the exchange
of pleasantries of townsfolk wafted in our ears.

Our eyes were focused on the deep blue sky well
above the puffy clouds that floated above us like cotton balls. We shared a pair of binoculars and an ex-
pandable telescope that we swapped back and forth.
We were looking for Russian airplanes, and we were
strategically located a stone's throw from the sheriff's office in case we needed to report invading
enemy aircraft.

World War II was fresh in everyone's mind, and
the Russians had recently launched Sputnik.
Increasing our fear were the school drills that were

intended to prepare us for a nuclear attack. On those occasions when the school bell rang four long rings, we hid under our desks until the "all clear bell" sounded with one long ring. If we were on the playground when the alarm rang, we had to lie flat on our stomachs until danger passed. Turnip was also located in tornado alley, and we did the same frightening drills for tornados.

With the preacher threatening hellfire and brimstone on the weekend, the school warning of incineration during the week, and the occasional tornado blowing us to kingdom come, it was a scary time to be a child.

Ben, the Air Force brat, knew a lot about airplanes and war because he was three years older and therefore smarter. That made me feel safe. He and I were Turnip's self-appointed civil air patrol.

Turnip was 100 miles from Dallas and 200 miles from Houston, so any plane that passed overhead was but a silver speck. The one exception was the U.S. military jet that had crashed about five miles out of town a couple of years before, leaving a big hole in Mr. McBride's field. Fortunately, the pilot had parachuted to safety.

"Ben, check out that plane! It looks kinda red to me. Do you think it's a Russian bomber?"

Ben snatched the dime store binoculars from me, and after a long study disappointedly said, "Naw, it looks like one of ours."

As we lay there awaiting the Russians, I wondered what would happen if they dropped a nuclear bomb on us. Would it kill us if we lay flat on the ground? I had seen the newsreels of how the blast

would blow apart and flatten buildings with huge winds and hot radioactive stuff.

"Ben, do you think the Russians will bomb us some-time?"

Ben thought for a moment, continuing to gaze into the sky and said, "Naw, they won't bomb Turnip. They don't care much about farmers." For the first time I felt good about being insignificant.

"If they bomb Dallas, do you think it will kill us?"

"Naw, it only kills stuff for fifty miles. It won't make it here unless they miss."

"How do you know that fifty-mile stuff?"

"Daddy told me," Ben confidently replied. "He's a sergeant in the Air Force, and he knows pretty much everything about that sorta stuff."

I felt easier as a high-flying buzzard entered our airspace.

"Buzzard!" I pointed. "You gotta watch him 'til he flaps his wings or it's bad luck."

He soon flapped and we rested, feeling good about having protected the country for one summer afternoon.

Life on the Skid

"Sing it, Jack!"

Each of Turnip's 381 citizens was like a cloth patch that when sewn together created a warm and cozy quilt that comforted me through my childhood. Jack Librand was one of the more beautiful patches.

Jack must have been forty years old—thirty years my senior—but stood no taller than I. As I faced Jack on a sunny October afternoon, I stood up straight and realized I had outgrown my first adult. I had inched up enough to look down into Jack's deep brown eyes, and I immediately felt uncomfortable doing so. It wasn't something I wanted to do, unlike Gib, the town bully, who seemed to enjoy towering over Jack and talking down to him in an artificially deep voice.

Jack was a kind and gentle soul who, if unfolded, would have been an exceptionally large man easily able to squish Gib into one of the cracks in the sidewalk where he surely belonged. Jack's problem wasn't his height. The problem was his legs. They didn't work.

Jack pulled himself beside my perch on the brick windowsill of the drug store for a visit. I was glad to see him. He flashed a genuine smile that exposed his oversized, tobacco-stained teeth and stuttered "H-H-H-Hi l-l-l-little H-H-H-Hank." Hank was my father's name, so the aristocracy connoted in "little Hank" struck me as a most pleasant greeting.

"Hey, Jack," came my reply.

Jack had arrived on his only transportation, which was unique in Turnip: a thick leather skid that turned up on three sides, forming a pouch for Jack's knees. His legs were eternally folded beneath his body, requiring him to sit on his feet. Jack grasped a wooden block in each hand that was about the size of a brick, with a thick wooden handle on top, so that by bending forward and placing the wooden block on the sidewalk in front of him, he could lift and pull himself along at a labored pace. The skid sounded like the rub of coarse sandpaper as it eked along the sidewalk.

Jack leaned back comfortably on his heels and removed his hands from the wooden blocks, crossing his arms. He began speaking in a terrible stutter that contorted his face almost to the point of pain. "H-H-H-How's it g-g-g-going, l-l-l-little H-H-H-Hank?"

"Fine," came my reply, as I unconsciously attempted to make up the time Jack had lost in his delivery. I knew I needed to carry the conversation to ease Jack's burden and that I should ask questions which could be answered in a simple "yep" or "nope." And if those words didn't come out, Jack could resort to a frustrated nod.

So I began, "Been doin' okay, Jack?"

"Y-Y-Y-Yep."

Then, "Been watchin' the Yankees whip the Dodgers in the Series, Jack?" I miscalculated. The question touched a chord close to Jack's Yankee heart, demanding more than a one-syllable answer.

"G-G-G-Goddamn, ain't that M-m-m-mick g-g-g-great!" he stammered over a forty-five-second period.

"He sure is, Jack. He's my hero."

It was good that I had plenty of time and nothing much to do because Jack needed an ear. Most adults weren't willing to work hard enough at listening or they were just too busy doing other things. I always liked visiting with Jack, hearing his concerns, sensing his emotions, and trying to figure out which vowels and consonants most jumbled his tongue.

I had not heard how Jack lost the use of his legs, and at ten, I was undaunted in asking. Jack blinked his brown eyes rapidly at not having addressed the question in a long time and began to answer.

"G-G-G-Goddamn t-t-t-tree g-g-g-got me," came his lengthy reply. "W-W-W-Was ch-ch-ch-chopping t-t-t-timber d-d-d-down by o-o-o-old man Ch-Ch-Ch-Chastain's s-s-s-sawmill for t-t-t-two dollars a day w-w-w-when this b-b-b-big old p-p-p-pine tr-tr-tr-tree sn-sn-sn-snapped early and I c-c-c-couldn't get o-o-o-out of the w-w-w-way." Almost a ten-minute sentence. (I thought of my grandfather, who said, "For all good things you have to wait.")

Jack continued with strained face and thick

tongue, attempting to maneuver the words out of his mouth accompanied by several saliva projectiles. "N-N-N-Nearly d-d-d-died that d-d-d-day. T-T-T-Took s-s-s-six m-m-m-men to get that g-g-g-goddamned t-t-t-tree off m-m-m-me. B-B-B-Broke my b-b-b-back, n-n-n-neck, and b-b-b-both l-l-l-legs. C-C-C-Crippled m-m-m-me from the w-w-w-waist d-d-d-down." He continued in labor, telling me he used to be 6'6", strong as a mule, but now he had no legs, no job, and no woman. He didn't want sympathy, but he also didn't like the hand he had been dealt.

I was about to ask my next question when Rudy Woods, the mechanic at Harper and Woods Garage, walked up with a big grin, rubbed my burr head, and shook Jack's hand. Jack's hand swallowed Rudy's hand as Jack stuttered and spit out a lengthy, "H-H-H-Hello, R-R-R-Rudy." Rudy characteristically carried the conversation for a while, with Jack nodding in Rudy's brief pauses.

As Rudy talked, I scrutinized Jack. He sat on his doubled-up withered legs with his black cowboy boots directly below his butt, toes pointing inward. He had his fixed blade hunting knife holstered on the left side of his belt. His western shirt was neatly ironed with his two top buttons undone, allowing plenty of room for a red handkerchief to wrap around his neck. Jack's coarse black hair was beginning to gray, but his straw cowboy hat hid any hint of a receding hairline. He was clean and closely shaven. His oversized wallet extended out of the back pocket of his jeans, exposing the chain that attached it to his belt loop. I was surprised to see a harmonica projecting from his shirt pocket but not surprised to see the yellow string and tab of his Prince Albert makings alongside.

As I turned back to their conversation, Rudy was humbly requesting Jack to perform one of his favorite country songs, *"I'm So Lonesome I Could Cry."* Jack attempted to say something, but the words were so difficult he finally yielded to his stutter and got out a quick "Yep" before the stutter could ruin that simple word, too.

He reached into his pocket, pulled out a silver harmonica inlaid with wood, and slapped it into the palm of his other hand as if to clear the dust out of its pipes. Confidently, he placed it between his lips and blew a test run of notes from one end to the other. He then took a deep breath, closed his eyes, and cradled the harmonica until it disappeared into his hands. The instrument didn't stutter a bit. Jack slid the harmonica across his mouth, opening and closing his hands to adjust the acoustics. A small crowd gathered. Jack's eyes remained closed as the downtowners were enraptured with his command of the instrument. When Rudy and the group began to clap in rhythm with the music, Jack opened his eyes and smiled. It shocked me when Rudy urged, "Sing it, Jack!"

I knew there was no way Jack could sing, and even if he could it would take a smooth hour for one song. But at that moment an incredible thing happened. Jack looked up and began to sing, "Did you ever see a night so long. . ." in a deep, rich baritone with not so much as a hint of a stutter. My eyes were big as silver dollars as I continued watching and listening to Jack sing as beautifully as any record I'd ever heard. More folks gathered in front of the drug store, softly clapping and moving gently to the rhythm. I was spellbound. When Jack sang the last note, everyone broke into applause and laughter. He was overcome with emotion, bowing his head several times.

Jack had amazed me and a few others in the crowd that day. I wondered if I had witnessed a miracle, like turning the water into wine, and if his stutter was cured. Then Jack said, "Th-Th-Th-Thank you," in what must have been forty syllables. And I knew nothing had changed other than my enlightenment.

I never figured out why Jack spoke with such difficulty yet sang with such ease. But I also never figured out how birds fly or fish breathe or flowers bloom. ✠

Hello Operator

"Someone had better be dead or dying."

The telephone system in Turnip was a close relative to the Pony Express. I picked up the heavy black telephone that had no dial or buttons, and after three rings Mrs. Minerva answered with "Central."

I lowered my voice to sound older and said, "Mrs. Minerva, may I talk to Tommy Turner please?"

She briskly replied, "Now, Cody, you know I'm busy and you don't need to be bothering me with idle chit-chat. If you want to talk to Tommy you just pedal yourself over to his house and talk as long as you want."

"Yes, ma'am." I hung up the phone and hopped on my bike. As I pedaled, I pondered Alexander Graham Bell and Mrs. Minerva.

We had only one telephone in our house—most did not have that. We were on a "party line" rather than the more expensive "private line," which meant five or six of our neighbors could pick up their phones and eavesdrop on our conversations. It also meant that if the neighbor was talking I would have to pick up the phone to see if she were finished before I could make a call. Of course, sometimes my curiosity bested me and I would listen until the neighbor admonished, "Now, I don't know who's listening but it's bad manners and you need to hang up," which I would quietly do.

Our phone only rang every couple of days. It was like an emergency device for adult communication to be used sparingly because of Mrs. Minerva. "Central" is what Mrs. Minerva called herself with varying inflection, depending on the kind of day she was having. The sole operator of the Turnip Telephone System, she lived only a couple of doors down from my house and sat facing the switchboard located in her home every day. It was a maze of plugs, holes, lights, and criss-crossed cords which she plugged and unplugged with the agility of an orchestra conductor. She wore a black headset that covered one ear with an accompanying mouthpiece curved in front of her sagging chin. While buzzers buzzed and lights flashed, she manually connected every phone call that was made in Turnip. She was also wondrously informed about community affairs.

After several occasions of watching Mrs. Minerva work, my amazement at her feats gave way to an understanding of why she was often short of patience—especially toward kids who sometimes forgot who they were calling by the time she answered the phone.

So, unless it was either an emergency or a test of

my ability to sound adult-like, I usually took the path of least resistance
and just yelled. Everyone in Turnip
kept their windows open day and
night except in winter, so voice communication was good and sometimes
superior to the phone system, which
shut down for dinner, for supper, and
for good at 9:00 P.M. If you needed to
make a call after that, you had to go
to Mrs. Minerva's home and bang on
the door loud enough to wake a hiber-
nating bear. She would come to the
door with droopy eyes in a well-worn
floor-length nightgown and consider
the intruder's special request. To be
sure, someone had better be dead or
dying, otherwise you were in for a
memorable experience.

Reading, Writing, and the Runs

"A chocolate double dipper, please."

I didn't realize that Papa couldn't read, and it didn't matter to me because I couldn't read either. We were doing fine without our reading skills until one day Papa decided to take me to town for an ice cream cone.

We got a cool drink from the dipper of well water and "struck-out-a-walkin'" on our one-mile jaunt to town. Soon Papa was carrying me, as usual, because my legs "wore plum out." He didn't mind the load. His back had carried far greater loads but none as important to him.

We arrived at the square in Turnip, which I always enjoyed. The town had a classical layout with a two-story brick courthouse in the center of the square, surrounded on four sides by brick and glass stores sporting canopies and benches. It was a town

150

that had made the transition from horses to cars comfortably but not completely and not without consternation.

Papa put me down on the sidewalk as we arrived in town. I was immediately caught up in the excitement of the people, cars, dogs, and storefront displays. Most people spoke as they met in Turnip because everyone knew each other, their parents, their grandparents, their social and economic standing, their moral fiber, and their religious convictions. Although we wore shoes, we walked carefully past the spit-and-whittle bench. The bench patrons were glad to see Papa because they enjoyed his stories. Hooker, they called him. Hooker Woodson. He was James Monroe Woodson, actually, but I didn't learn his formal name until years later.

When we arrived at Bull's Drug Store, a disastrous sequence of events began to unfold that made me realize that an education wasn't all bad. The drug store had a large plate glass window overlooking the only intersection in town deserving a blinking traffic light. Inside the door below the window was a selection of hundreds of comic books strewn and tattered from browsing. Beyond the comics were scales which for one penny and a turn of the dial would reveal your weight as well as the secrets of your future. Walking past the scales, we approached the marble soda fountain counter which Mrs. Wade tended while standing on a raised wooden platform. She looked eight feet tall back there, even though she was no taller than my grandfather. She asked in a stern voice with an unwavering eye, "What can I get you, young man?" We were regulars in the drug store and Mrs. Wade knew us, but she was short on small talk. My grandfather boosted me up on his knee and my eyes scanned the assorted cups, glasses, and stainless steel holders reflected in the mirror. Mrs. Wade's admonitions had taught me to hurry up and decide, so I ordered my usual—"A chocolate double dipper, please."

As I sat on the stool eating my ice cream, I could see the prescription counter where Bull Johnson was busy counting pills. I shuddered. That was the same counter that doubled as a shield when Bull decided to play doctor and give shots to children restrained by parents. I remembered being terrorized there more than once. Bull would say, "Now, pull his pants down and hold him good. Have you got him?" Seeing his gleaming needle that looked long enough to go completely through my body, I would begin to scream and squirm wildly until Bull had the needle so close that the danger of his missing and breaking off the needle frightened me more than getting the shot. So I would stiffen like a board and pray he wouldn't hit a bone. At that moment he always had the audacity to say, "Now, this won't hurt!" as he thrust the needle all the way in. I wouldn't watch the jab, but I would watch in horror as he pulled the needle out to be sure it was still in one piece. Bull would then rub the spot with an alcohol cotton ball and smile as he watched me hop like I was on a pogo stick as I held my wound.

I tried to never be sick enough to need a shot. After my first puncture from Bull, the smell of the drug store was imprinted on me for life. For the rest of my days, entering the drug store was much like the reaction my dog had when he entered the vet's office. I understood the look in my dog's eye. Actually, Bull was happy to practice his craft on dogs, too. Nothing was sacred to Bull Johnson.

Well, Papa and I had finished our business, and it was time to leave the drug store when I spotted an item I knew we could afford. I looked straight up at my Papa with sad brown eyes and convinced him that a box of chewing gum would be good for the trip home.

Papa was a man of little money, but he tried to buy me everything he could afford. He, too, thought the gum as a good idea, even though he had no interest in gum and no teeth to chew with, so we paid up and left.

We were dressed in matching striped bib overalls and high top shoes, which Papa called brogans. As we walked on the edge of the paved two-lane, encountering only an occasional car, our conversation was lively as Papa let me eat the entire box of gum. It tasted funny but chewed good.

Well, by the time I got to the house I was having serious stomach problems. As it turned out, the box of gum that neither Papa nor I could read the name of was not gum at all. It was Feenamint Laxative. A dosage like I had just taken was enough to ruin an adult, not to mention what it did to my five-year-old body.

Mama and Papa both cried with me for the next few hours. Papa identified the problem as "the runs," which sounded right to me. No one ever had to explain diarrhea or laxatives to me after that day. Later in life, when I was able to stand again, I realized that Papa was as sick as I had been over the incident and suffered his mistake far longer. 🎟

End of the World

"Those red hot stars looked like they might be brimstone falling from heaven."

Summer was dying. Only a few sweet days remained before school started, bringing with it hard new blue jeans, tight shoes, heavy books, and homework. It was late August and scalding hot when Ben and I decided on one last overnight campout in my big backyard. Little did we know the world was coming to an end that very evening.

Afternoon faded to warm evening as Ben and I sat Indian-style not too close to our brick-lined campfire. Lightning bugs danced about us like UFOs flashing their signals. Cicadas hummed from their hidden perches in the surrounding pecan trees that were beginning to take on the form of giant creatures. As the flame flickered in Ben's thick glasses, I was glad not to be alone in the gathering darkness and glad that Ben was twelve—three years older than I.

Earlier in the day, Ben and I had pulled a beast-sized fallen tree limb from the front yard to the middle of the backyard so our hideout and campfire would be open to the big sky above. We had sculpted the leafy pecan limb into a hut with our hatchets and knives, creating places to prop our protective BB guns and hang our canvas canteens and smelly kerosene lantern. We had made our door from an old towel, and we had borrowed one of Mother's not-so-old sheets for groundcover, realizing there would be a price to pay the following day. When the cave was complete, we tried it out. There was enough room for us and maybe my tired old dog Blackie, too. We were prepared for anything, except what was to come out of the sky.

Darkness was everywhere as we fed the green scraps we'd cut off the giant limb into the campfire, its embers rising and vanishing in the thick night air. Ben and I sat opposite each other and waged war over the crackling fire with our hot dogs impaled on forked sticks. When we had eaten our fill of burned hot dogs and ashes and gooey black marshmallows and told more than a few jokes and scary stories, we lay on our backs to survey heaven.

It must have been midnight. All the lights in the surrounding houses were out and had been since 10:00 or so. Downtown was only a block away, but the stores had closed before dark, and Turnip couldn't afford streetlights. The moon was on vacation, and the night was as dark as Chili McMillan's skin.

As we lay side by side, looking up with our bare feet enjoying the cushioned St. Augustine grass, the stars twinkled as bright as Christmas, and the Milky

Way was more vivid than I had ever seen. Suddenly, a shooting star appeared. Ben stopped his story about the two boys in Evansville who were kidnapped and decapitated by a stranger or a monster. Ben said, "Wow, look at that star—make a wish!" I was nine and there was plenty to wish for, so I closed my eyes and envisioned a shiny new red bicycle with a light and a horn and, yes, why not a speedometer?

I opened my eyes with a smile, and another star fell as I said to Ben, "That's yours. You make a wish." I watched as Ben closed his eyes for a long time. I guessed that twelve-year-olds had even more to wish for. As we lay looking up and talking about our wishes, more stars shot across the sky. "Ben, I haven't seen this many shooting stars in my whole life, have you?"

"No," Ben said soberly. "This is really weird."

"Where do you think those stars are landing?" I asked with a little concern.

"I don't know. That last one looked like it was headed toward Dallas." At that moment, a huge star streaked across the sky. "Wow," we said in unison.

"That one is headed toward Houston," Ben said knowingly from his tenure as an Air Force brat.

Then eight or ten streaked at almost the same time.

"Ben, are those stars, or could they be rocket ships from outer space?"

Trying to sound definitive and older, Ben said, "Naw, those are just shooting stars." He paused. "I just can't believe there are so many of them."

"Ben, could one of those stars land on us?"

Ben's pause told me plenty. "I don't think so," he hesitantly replied.

I thought about the preacher who had told us three times a week that one day the world would come to an end with hellfire and brimstone falling on the unjust, and that we needed to repent and be saved. I didn't know what "repent" meant, but I was beginning to feel the need to be saved. I didn't know what brimstone was either, but those red hot stars looked like they might be brimstone falling from heaven. I knew Ben didn't go to church, and he might be more of a target than I was. Brimstone began streaking across the sky with increasing intensity.

"Ben, let's go inside the hideout," I urged.

"Okay," Ben immediately replied, leading the way into the hideout on all fours.

Blackie raised his head but didn't budge, then returned his head to the ground with a soft groan and a sigh of unconcern.

The leaves were like camouflage, but the stars filled every hole in the ceiling. Stars streaked as we worried in silence. Finally I asked what I really feared, "Ben, is the sky falling?" Ben hesitated again, and my breathing accelerated.

"It couldn't," Ben deduced, but his voice betrayed him.

I rolled on my side, facing Ben directly, and in controlled panic said, "Is this the end of the world, Ben?"

Ben swallowed, his gaze not turning from the heavens. "I hope not."

My mind was now on full terror alert. Monsters and kidnappers were not a concern. My eternal soul was a concern, and my young life was a huge concern. I was no longer afraid to show my state of complete fright.

"Let's go inside the house, Ben. The roof on the house is strong, and Daddy will know what to do if a star hits the house."

Ben paused, but not for long. "Okay, I'll go with you."

I didn't buy his I'm-not-afraid-but-I-know-you-are routine. I threw open the towel door, and Ben was less than a step behind when we opened the back screen door and were enveloped in the safety of the house with the nearby presence of my dad.

We crawled under the sheet of my twin bed, dirty feet and all, with my brother Jim sound asleep in the other one. Ben and I were squinched up side by side, and that was fine with me. His warm and larger body felt good. I looked toward the ceiling in the pitch-black room. No stars, thank God. I listened for crashing stars nearby but heard none. Ben's breathing, which was beginning to slow, and Daddy's distant snore were all I heard. I wondered if Blackie would be okay outside. He had seemed unconcerned as Ben and I had high-tailed it for the house.

It was late. Sleep overtook us.

I awoke first the next morning. I felt my chest. I

was alive. No burns. No bruises. The ceiling had no holes. I supposed the world had not come to an end. Ben's glasses were on the nightstand and his mouth was open as he breathed deeply. Jim was asleep also. I eased out of bed and tiptoed to the kitchen table still dressed in my T-shirt and shorts in case I had to make a run for it.

Mother and Daddy were sitting at the breakfast table having coffee, with Daddy hidden behind the newspaper. Daddy peeked over the paper with a nod and Mother greeted me with a cheerful but inquisitive, "Good morning, Cody. I thought you two were outside camping?"

I told her my story in gulps as Daddy rested the paper and listened. The more I talked, the more Daddy seemed to enjoy my story. When I finished, Daddy's face was in an uncharacteristic full smile. He turned the front page toward me and showed me the headlines: PERSEID METEOR SHOWER BEST IN YEARS.

Paperboy

*"If all else failed, I stared at them with my big brown
eyes and looked pitiful. Pity was probably
my most effective approach."*

The first wobbling steps of my business career
were taken at age eight. Eddie Sanders was retiring
from his paper route, and my brother Jim and I took
it over. That was to be our first encounter with John
Q. Public up close and personal.

Jim and I split the route. I took downtown and
close to the square, while Jim, being older, pedaled
the highways. He complained little for the extra load
that he certainly carried, even when it was the end
of the month and time to 50-50 the profits. I was
lucky in more ways than one to get the downtown
route because I enjoyed interacting with the store-
keepers and downtowners, which obviously couldn't
be done while pedaling the roads and dodging cars
and bad dogs.

Our motive from day one was profit. We had seen
Eddie's pockets bulge with nickels, and we knew the

161

purchasing power and opportunities they would provide. No longer would we have to wait for a big
spender to toss a half-cent Coke bottle out his car
window into the ditch for us to be able to earn a
Coke or candy bar. Visions of riches danced in our
heads. Mother and Daddy told us the money would
be ours to use as we saw fit, within certain guide-
lines, but they made it clear the responsibility of the
job fell solely on our shoulders. Their exhortations
sailed over our heads as we visualized the previously
unaffordable banana splits that could now be ours,
not to mention pocketknives or pinball games. We
were primed and ready.

The post office was our headquarters and the
place where the *Dallas Times Herald* man dropped
off our tightly bundled forty or so newspapers. On
the first day two new canvas saddlebags for our bicycles were also delivered, along with a sleeve of tiny
copper wires to bind the rolled-up papers. The bill
for our new equipment, payable on or before the
tenth of the following month, came as a surprise.

Jim and I dragged the heavy papers inside the
post office. Eddie had told us this was "public
space" and could be used for rolling our papers.
Well, it didn't take thirty seconds for the postmaster
to set us straight about whose floor we were using
and what condition he expected us to leave it in.
Furthermore, he stated there would be no dogs or
bikes inside the concrete floored lobby that he
swept. This was the first sign that maybe Eddie had
not told us everything about the newspaper business.

Under the postmaster's wary gaze, we began to

try to wrap the newspapers into tight rolls, twisting a copper wire to bind each one. Although we'd watched Eddie do it instantly and effortlessly, our first wrapping required more time than the delivery. And the delivery would not have taken nearly so long had the papers not exploded on impact, requiring a chase to recover the sections blowing across lawns. Also, as I learned from more than one person that first entrepreneurial day, newspapers were not to be wrapped for delivery to stores but were to be laid neatly in the precise location that Eddie had delivered them for the past several years. I learned, too, that the new-smelling saddlebag pouch I had purchased with as-yet no income was unnecessary for my around-town route. Walking with fresh newspapers neatly aligned under my arm was the only way to go. I did wonder about the black stuff that was all over my hands and once-white T-shirt. Mother was not going to be happy.

The *Times Herald* was the daily afternoon newspaper and was also delivered on Sunday morning before church. "Daily" was a word I did not fully appreciate before the paper route. I soon realized that daily meant *every* day. It didn't take long to learn the harsh reality that the newspaper took no holidays. Rain or shine, tired or sick, in my nine years of delivering the paper, the carrier never failed to make his drop. Never. Not once. Not even Christmas! A man was in the making, which was more than I had bargained for: all I wanted was money and ice cream and bulging pockets. However, my education was just beginning.

My brother soon retired from this public work

and engaged in the private enterprise of lawn mowing. His flexible hours, high pay, and seasonal work were enviable. But Daddy said I was too young for a mower and that I needed to stick with the job I had.

It was midsummer, and I had been a paperboy for about a month. I rolled my papers on the wide concrete sidewalk in the shade of the post office sitting beside my newspaper stand, which was a flimsy wire rack for a dozen or so papers with a slotted red cylinder to the side for change. Payment was on the honor system—5¢ daily, 20¢ Sunday. When week after week my totals from the coin bin were never divisible by 5¢, I learned something about human nature. The quantity of money in the cylinder was not large, but it was my livelihood; and each 5¢ paper cost me 3¢. I decided not to unlock and empty the change bin every week so it would seem like more profit when I did. After almost three weeks of waiting, I turned to deposit my papers in the rack only to find that the rack was gone—not moved, stolen! A second lesson about human nature. I promptly invested in the hardware store's best lock and chain, attaching my livelihood to a telephone pole in front of the post office. I wasn't going to wait for human nature's third revelation.

I soon calculated that if I had

more customers, I could make more profit. So I decided to go knock on a few doors. I remembered my father's advice, "Son, look people in the eye when you shake hands with them. Shake hands firmly and speak pleasantly, distinctly, and with confidence. Keep your shoes shined, your teeth brushed, your hair combed, and your fingernails clean. And dress neatly. How you look will tell people things about you that words can't."

Following my dad's advice, I began knocking firmly and persistently on doors. Before noon on my first day of trying to get more customers, I was exposed to more personality types than I had ever imagined existed. These people had more excuses for not subscribing than I could have ever dreamed up in all eight years of my life. I was also surprised at my ability to detect untruth and dishonesty—qualities I hadn't expected from grown-ups. My dad had taught me that "a man's word is his bond," and that every aspect of life depended on honesty. He said, "Tell people what you're going to do and do what you tell them. Don't sell what you can't deliver!" He also told me, "You're not selling a product—you're selling yourself." Well, I soon learned most of the world didn't live by Daddy's standards.

After many rejections, I tried new approaches to selling. Sizing up the customer for the best approach was the real challenge. Some folks said they couldn't afford the $1.70 per month cost, to which I offered the five-day-a-week option or the Sunday-only option. Other folks weren't convinced of my capabilities, to which I offered my satisfaction-guaranteed-or-money-back option. Then others needed to be convinced of my need for their business, in which case I used the approach that it was good to reward industriousness. And, if all else failed, I stared at them with my big brown eyes and looked pitiful. Pity was probably my most effective approach.

Getting business was one thing. Taking care of business was quite another. Before my paper route, nothing in my life was on a schedule except school. The burden of my seven-day-a-week responsibilities became apparent to me when, in about week six of my newspaper career, I simply forgot to deliver the papers. Five o'clock rolled around, and people began to call. I had to answer. I soon learned that excuses won't get the job done, but a sincere apology and swift action will. From that experience I learned to keep my mind on my business and to put my customers' concerns before my own. I also discovered that for the most part, if I treated people right, they would treat me right. That was lesson three of human nature, and I liked it. That left me more in charge. I did my best to treat people right. Only on a few occasions did I actually try to throw someone's paper in the dog shit in the yard.

It's difficult to think of a way for a boy to learn more about people and life than through being a paperboy. Even though my parents had enough money for my brother and me not to work, they realized the value in working for the public. Their hunch of what that experience would do for me was right on target, even though they often cringed at my learning experiences.

I encountered almost every personality type in delivering the papers. I met industrious people and deadbeats, lonely people, sick people, disturbed people, happy people, mean people, and old people. Some were full of love, some full of hate, some full of themselves, and some full of nothing. I also learned something about being all things to all people so long as I didn't compromise my father's values. And I learned at least as much from bad experiences as good ones. I was cussed at, lied to, cheated, and praised. I cried some and got mad some, but mostly I matured. I had doors slammed in my face and doors opened for me. Such is life.

For an innocent church-going boy of eight, I learned lessons about human nature and life that are with me still. 🌺

Fast Money

*"Dewey came around the corner and
caught us red-handed."*

Dewey's Filling Station was a fine place for boys.
I was always welcome as long as I didn't get in the
way when Dewey was busy or out of sorts.

Dewey and his black helper, Lester, genuinely enjoyed my company as we sat on wooden Coke boxes
while they told jokes and were amused by my
naiveté. They tried to keep their cussing down while
I was there because they knew Mother didn't approve. Laughter was always close at hand for Lester.
When he laughed, he would lean back on his Coke
box and cover his mouth with his hand so as not to
expose his missing teeth or the smell of liquor often
on his breath. I spent many happy hours at Dewey's
listening to philosophy while sitting on those
wooden Coke boxes.

Dewey made Lester fix my bicycle flats because
Dewey hated working on skinny tubes with his fat
fingers. And Lester would usually let me patch my

own because he hated them, too. Boy, what fun! The smell of achievement in melting those Monkey Grip patches as they vulcanized to the inner tube was breathtaking. I loved to watch it smoke. Dewey would usually stay outside while I used his equipment because he hated that, too.

Dewey was a fat man in his fifties who wore gray pants and matching shirt with his name in red cursive stitching above the Gulf logo. He wore wide suspenders which were overworked, as were his lace-up boots. His hair was mostly gone, but his eyesight was not. He carried a wad of cash in his bulging wallet that would sink a small boat. Dewey was friendly as he slowly serviced every car that drove into his one covered bay and two-pump station. He chain-smoked Camels even while gassing up cars, usually keeping the cigarette in the same hand as the nozzle. In retrospect, I'm amazed there was never an explosion and fire. He and Lester kept the concrete clean with their high-pressure hose, with extra sprayings on hot summer days. The tiny office of the station had no air conditioner but did have a small, open-flame gas heater for winter.

Lester was a small, thin black man of unknown age with a few sprinkles of gray in his closely cropped hair. He had worked for Dewey long enough to have a gray shirt like Dewey's with his name on it as well. Lester moved fluidly around the station as if his bones were rubber. Quick to smile and slow to anger, he got along fine with us boys.

Dewey's was located one block off the square. The metal sign standing out front between the station and Highway 79 announced that gasoline was

27¢ per gallon. That didn't interest me in the least. What did interest me was Dewey's ice cream box, the coldest one in town. It was a big white box with chrome doors on top that when lifted revealed a thick layer of frost inside. It was high enough that I had to jump up on the side and lean half my body down inside the smoking box with my legs and black-bottomed bare feet dangling outside. Dewey didn't like for the box lid to stay open long and usually offered to help with my selection. That idea was inconceivable to me because I had to see and mentally taste all my choices every time to be sure I got exactly the right one. I knew Dewey was a smart man because he had the best selection in town: chocolate and banana Fudgesicles; grape, strawberry, orange, and lime Popsicles (the kind with two wooden sticks that did not stick to the wrapper); Eskimo pies; Neapolitan ice cream sandwiches; and strawberry pushups on a round pointed stick. Any selection was a nickel—the same as Cokes.

But the best part of Dewey's ice cream box was that it contained the coldest, hardest, chocolatiest candy in town. During summer, at all other stores in town, the Butterfingers slid out of the wrapper with no chocolate on them, the M&Ms melted before they got into your hands, and I had to lick the Hershey's chocolate bar off the foil wrapper. But not at Dewey's. He kept 'em cold and liked to eat 'em cold.

Most significantly for me, Dewey would also buy back empty Coke bottles for a half cent apiece. This was most often my primary source of spending money—that is, until the time that my older friend Ben figured out that if we were careful we could get the Coke bottles from around back and bring them to the front of the station and collect fast money with much less effort than cleaning all the ditches in town!

Well, old Dewey wasn't as dumb as we thought. After bringing an increasingly larger supply of bottles three days in a row, Dewey came around the corner and caught us red-handed, loading bottles into the baskets on our bicycles. Dewey turned beet red, and the cussing started. He used words I had never heard. I felt guilty and embarrassed almost to the point of crying. Ben was just sorry we got caught.

Needless to say, I didn't mention the cussing to Mother and prayed that Dewey would not mention the stealing. I distinctly remember the next time I went to Dewey's Filling Station and the feeling in the bottom of my stomach as Daddy drove up to the pump. I slumped in the passenger seat as my eyes met Dewey's. I knew if he spilled the beans to Daddy, I would not receive one of Mother's searing lectures—I would be beaten to death. Dewey's eyes told me that he knew that, too. He spared me.

I owed him one, and I never forgot.

The Silver Gun

*"I knew that my grandfather would buy me anything
I really wanted."*

The toy gun in the glass case at the drug store
captured my desire and imagination more than anything I had ever wanted. Every time I went to town
I made a bee line for the drug store and pressed my
nose to the glass case to get as close as I could to the
gun. I just knew that if I could own that gun I would
be completely happy for the rest of my life.

A large, silver-colored six-shooter with pearl handles, the gun came with bullets that could be removed from the cylinder. Each bullet could be taken
apart and a round "cap" placed inside so that when
the trigger was pulled, the gun sounded and smelled
real. The silver gun looked just like the one the Lone
Ranger carried. It was beautiful and perfect. I envisioned myself watching TV with my gun and shooting the bad guys.

The gun cost $3.95, including holster, belt, and
extra bullets. I begged Mother on several occasions

for the gun, even with tears, but she was careful and practical with our money, and the six-gun was just another toy to her. She was simply incapable of grasping the importance of that gun. She wouldn't even allow Bull to get it out of the case so I could touch it.

I was not going to ask Daddy for the gun because he had just returned from fighting the Germans, and he hated guns. Furthermore, if Daddy said no, the discussion was ended forever, unless I wanted a whipping to go along with the "no."

Then came the breakthrough—my grandfather. I knew that my grandfather would buy me anything I really wanted if he could afford it. Unlike my parents, he could tell what was important to me. The only problem was that he had almost no money. He didn't own a car or a house, didn't have a checking account, had retired from his job as janitor of the courthouse, and depended on a small government check or Mother to supply his needs.

I pleaded with Mother one final time to buy me the gun, but her refusal was emphatic. So, later that day I left a note for Mother, sneaked out of the

house, and walked the mile to my grandparents'
house, something I had never done before and something Mother would never have allowed. I cried as I
told Papa my story. He went to his cigar box on the
dresser and got his folding money that he kept
"salted away for a rainy day." He came back to the
living room and said in a worried tone, "Okay, Cody,
let's go get that gun."

I could already feel how great it would be to walk
out of the drug store with the shiny silver gun
strapped to my hip. But I also began to feel a gnaw-
ing guilt for running away from home and more than
a little shame for manipulating Papa into buying a
gun with what little money he had.

Any remorse faded as we walked to town. I
pulled Papa to the glass case in the drug store and,
thank goodness, the gun was still there. I ran to the
window where Bull counted pills and told him we
needed help and that I was going to buy the silver
gun. Bull craned his neck to see who the purchaser
was. He looked back at me over his glasses and said,
"Young man, does your mother know you're buying
the gun?"

"No, sir."

Bull stared at me a moment, contemplating the
situation, then went to the case, opened it, and
handed me the whole rig.

"Hooker, are you buying this for Cody?" Bull was
well aware of Papa's financial situation.

"Yeah, the boy needs that gun. His mama won't
buy it for him, so I guess I will. She's gonna throw a
fit." They both nodded, agreeing that they would
also be in for some kind of retribution. We paid up,

and I strapped the gun on and put the roll of caps that Bull had donated into my pocket.

Papa said I had to go back to my house and that he would walk me. When we got to the house, Mother was standing in the screen door, waiting with her hand on her hip and holding my note in the other hand. She looked at the gun, looked at Papa, and then at me. She didn't throw a fit, but she gave me a look that was much worse.

Papa hugged me and left to walk home. Mother silently went about her chores, leaving me with the gun.

I went to my room, sat on the floor, and excitedly loaded all six cylinders with caps as well as the bullets in the gun belt. I started pulling the trigger like the Lone Ranger, but only one of the six shots fired. I pulled the trigger a dozen more times. Nothing happened. I reloaded with new bullets and pulled the trigger again. Nothing. I opened the cylinder and it fell to the floor. I pushed the cylinder back in place and noticed the pearl handles were loose. Then I realized the gun wasn't as heavy or as shiny as I had remembered.

I never divulged that the gun was anything other than perfect. I would think a lot about that year of wanting, begging for, and buying the gun. Happiness never came, but a lesson did. ❧

Salty Bird

*"My nose began to itch. I didn't scratch. I needed a drink.
I stealthily licked my lips, which tasted of salt,
and waited."*

I was eight years old and smitten with the idea of catching a bird and teaching him tricks. I asked my grandfather for advice. He smiled and sent me out of his house with a salt shaker and these words, "You know, if you sprinkle salt on a bird's tail, he can't fly." I assumed salt worked something like kryptonite. So, with salt shaker in hand, I chased birds on the ground, showering them with my shaker. They flew. Then I pitched salt on birds in trees. They flew. Ultimately I chunked the entire shaker at birds. They flew. It seemed my only accomplishment was making my Papa's yard look like it had the mange.

I was beginning to wonder if salting a bird's tail was in the same category as the tooth fairy, haints, and snipes. I decided on one last, calculated attempt.

I walked to the courthouse where the flat-topped

hedges chirped like a parakeet store and advanced toward my target with a full supply of ammunition in a round Morton's salt box. I crouched as I made my way toward the loudest hedge. I could see sparrows hopping briskly from limb to limb. The hedge emptied on my arrival. No surprise. I selected my position and poured myself an overflowing handful of salt, then stood like the Statue of Liberty, committed to the birds' return.

The afternoon sun soon began taking its toll on the statue. Sweat was running into my eyes. I didn't wipe. My nose began to itch. I didn't scratch. I needed a drink. I stealthily licked my lips, which tasted of salt, and waited.

About seventy-nine hours later the hedge had refilled with dozens of jittery sparrows who must have thought I was a rain forest tree. I allowed myself a faint smile. My face was directly above the hedge and less than two feet from the colony of birds. I could see their bulging brown eyes rapidly glancing about and their little gray eyelids punctuating each blink. They fluttered their wings and twitched their tails, conversing like a family reunion. The numb arm that supported my raised hand was ready. It was D-Day for the inhabitants of the waist-high hedge. I let fly with a million grains of salt as I watched with microscopic attention. The salt sounded like sand pelting a windowpane as it bombed the hedge, landing on heads, wings, and, yes, tails. It missed nothing, and this time I was sure.

Suddenly the salt-drenched birds burst from the hedge, wildly flapping their wings against my face and arms. My eyes slammed shut and my head recoiled as I fell backward. I hit the ground, opening my eyes, and rolled to my stomach. My chin was stationary on the ground as my eyes scanned the dirt. No paralyzed birds. I quickly rose to a crouch, placing my face against the leaves as my eyes searched the limbs. No paralyzed birds. I backed from the hedge and opened my tactical hand—only a small amount of wet salt. No birds.

I dusted off my hands and stooped to pick up my box of salt. The hedges chirped with laughter as the birds flitted about. I wiped my face, tasting salt again.

Then I thought of Papa and smiled. I could just see him rocking on the front porch, totally amused.

Black and White

"Do colored people have black blood or red blood?"

I walked into Hill's Lumber Hardware and Undertaking to inspect the knives, lures, and BB guns. My bare feet liked the smooth, creaking wood floor, my eyes liked the tall walls neatly stocked with hardware, and my nose certainly liked the conglomerated smells of lumber, metal, rubber, and paint. It was also the closest thing to a toy store in Turnip.

Dave, Mrs. Hill's helper, who was standing on the rolling ladder with feather duster in hand, turned to greet me with a smile. "Hello, young man. What can I do you for?" He made his way down the ladder and extended his strong black hand. We shook. He seemed happy to have a customer.

"I'm just lookin', Dave. Got anything new?"

"Not since yesterday," he laughed heartily.

I blushed, having forgotten that it had only been one day since my last visit. I looked around and noticed Mrs. Hill was not in the store as Dave, already walking toward my favorite glass case, asked, "Wanna see some knives?"

"Yes, sir," I said enthusiastically, following him to the knife and fishing lure case, surprised that he had read my mind.

Dave was a smart man with an athletic build, a sparkle in his eye, a quick wit, and an easy smile. He had the beginnings of gray in his short kinky hair and dressed neatly in khaki pants, freshly ironed shirt, and thick-soled work shoes.

Dave slid the glass door open from the proprietor side of the counter and reached for a beautiful, yellow-handled pocketknife cushioned with cotton in its elongated box. He carefully opened the largest of three blades and handed me the knife, handle first. As I grasped the smooth handle and carefully removed the knife from his hand, I noticed that his washpot black hand was lily white on the inside with dark wrinkle lines.

I raised my left hand to the blade and tested the sharpness as I read the name aloud, "Shrade."

"Yes, sir, that's a fine piece of steel," Dave advised.

"It's a beauty." I carefully opened and closed each blade, finally sliding the knife into my pocket to see what owning the knife felt like.

"You borrowin' or buyin' today?" Dave chuckled.

I quickly handed the knife back to Dave. "Just lookin'," I offered, a little embarrassed.

Dave replaced the knife and brought out another whose brown and white handle resembled tree bark. We must have looked at a dozen more knives, including two fixed-blade hunting knives with leather sheaths that Dave patiently helped me attach to the belt on my blue jeans.

Dave was a rare breed in Turnip as he had an almost white-collar job. No business owner in Turnip was black. No teacher or student in my school was black. No Christian in my church was black. Certainly no lawyer, judge, or sheriff was black. Farm hands were black. Laborers were black. Cooks, maids, and a few storehands were black if they were humble, mannerly, and extremely capable. Such was the case with Dave.

Dave returned to dusting with, "You take your time lookin' and let me know if you need help." He had read my mind again, probably knowing I didn't have the $2.75 to purchase the yellow-handled knife of my dreams.

"Yes, sir," I answered appreciatively as I pondered Dave and Turnip.

Most white people in Turnip called black people "niggers." Mother and Daddy taught me to treat people with respect regardless of color, but the town did not abide by that standard. Turnip's central building, the courthouse, which represented law and order and justice, stated the sentiment of the white community perfectly with the signs above the two public drinking fountains, located in the corridor adjacent to the sheriff's office. The clean stainless steel one with chilled water read "Whites Only." The orange-stained, porcelain, low-pressure fountain read "Colored." The restrooms had the same designations. I assumed coloreds had diseases we could catch.

The City Cafe was the only restaurant in Turnip. Blacks not only couldn't eat with whites, they

weren't allowed in the front door. They could, however, come to the back door and buy food or eat free
leftovers that Dave's wife, Lilah, was plentiful with.
There was another class, a small class, of what some
white folks called "uppity niggers." They were
bright, well-educated people who held their heads
high, didn't speak in dialect, drove better cars, and
lived in better houses than many whites. These
blacks were resented by most whites for not "knowing their place." It was the South. Civil rights issues
were no closer than the Civil War. *Brown vs. Board of
Education* was unheard of, as was Dr. Martin Luther
King, Jr.

Dave sat down in one of the customer chairs beside Mrs. Hill's desk and gestured with his hand,
"Have a sit." I accepted. We talked of hunting and
fishing, baseball and football, school and church.
Dave did most of the listening. It was
the most conversation we ever had.
His questions showed an interest in
my view of the white perspective.
My nine-year-old curiosity felt liber-
ated enough for the first time to ask
some questions that had always
troubled me.

"Dave, why are some black people blacker than others?"

Dave was surprised by the question. "Well, I don't rightly know. I
guess . . . I guess it's just the way
God painted us."

I continued. "But some black
people have freckles and green eyes,

and some have skin that's almost clear and eyes that look like dead people."

Dave smiled at my intensity. "You pay attention, don't you, boy?" He rubbed his chin and jaw as he replied. "Let's see . . . the green eyes and freckles . . . I suppose those came from some slave owner way back when. We call the really light-colored folks albinos because they don't have much color in their skin or their eyes." He smiled. "They look a little strange to me, too."

I shifted in my chair. "Okay, Dave, how about blood? Do colored people have black blood or red blood?"

Dave began to laugh. "Oh, boy, you're killing me." He paused, then asked, "Well, do you have white blood or red blood?" Shaking his head side to side, he said more seriously, "My blood is as red as yours."

I felt better.

"Dave, back to the color thing. Your hands are black on the outside and white on the inside and your face is black on the outside but the inside of your mouth is pink. Does the black rub off?"

Dave slapped his knee and bent over. "Where do you get these ideas, boy?"

"I don't know," I replied. "I just wonder."

"Well, it doesn't rub off." He inspected his hands, turning them over a couple of times. "But I guess it does look like it," he added thoughtfully.

I continued, hoping to get all the answers in one whack. "Why do all colored people have kinky hair? Do you curl it?"

"Naw, boy. This is the way God made us," he said, pulling off his baseball cap and rubbing his head. He read my mind again when he offered, "Want to feel it?" bending his head down.

I hesitantly placed my hand on his head. It felt like spring wire. "That's funny feelin', Dave."

He raised his head, smiling, then rubbed my burr head and said, "That's funny feelin', too." We both laughed.

I sobered. "Dave, why do white people call black people 'niggers'?"

Dave stopped smiling. I sensed pain as he replied, "Son, 'nigger' is a bad word, and I don't want to ever hear you say it." He paused taking a deep breath, "'Nigger' is what slaves were called. Black people aren't slaves anymore, but most white folk act like they are. I'd best leave it at that."

"Do you like being colored, Dave?" I asked innocently.

"Whew," blowing air out his large lips, "that's about enough questions for one day, Cody."

I realized I'd gone either too far or too long. "Yes, sir, I didn't mean any harm."

"I know, boy," Dave said, rising from his chair. "I know your parents. They're good people. A sight better than most. No harm, boy. Maybe some good. You come back, and maybe we'll talk another day."

I then realized Dave feared that maybe he had gone too far—just like if he had decided to sit in Mrs. Hill's chair.

As we headed to the door, I offered, "Dave, I won't tell anybody about this if you won't."

He smiled, placing a reassuring hand on my shoulder, "Okay, Cody, deal." We shook on what was to be our only discussion of black and white.

Small-Town White Lie

*"If city folks find out you're from a small town,
they'll take advantage of you."*

Turnip was too small a town for a clothing store,
so Mother drove me to the city of Evansville (pop.
11,230) to purchase my first suit. I was eleven years
old, and Mother thought it high time that I was
properly dressed for church. Although she'd been
waiting for years for my growth spurts to subside,
she finally gave up and we went shopping.

We walked into a department store that adver-
tised clothing for men and boys. The store was big
and tall with wood floors, and it smelled of oil and
contained everything a body could want—from
shirts and slacks to shoes, ties, belts, hats, suspenders, and racks and racks of suits of all sizes.

A tall, thin, funeral home-looking fellow greeted
us with folded arms as Mother thumbed the price
tags on the suit sleeves. "May I help you, ma'am?"
the undertaker greeted us with a rehearsed smile.

Mother eyed him from top to bottom, deciding he would do. "Yes, sir, my son needs a suit."

He dipped his head and beamed, "You've come to the right place, ma'am. We have an excellent selection of suits that would fit your son to a T," adding with a wink, "and good prices to boot. Let's try one on for size." He slid a silky black suit off the hanger. As he helped me into the jacket, one arm at a time, the salesman attempted to bond with Mother. "Where are you folks from, ma'am?"

Not liking the invasion, Mother replied, "Turnip," in a tone that suggested he not tread further.

He didn't get the hint. "Turnip . . . Turnip . . . I don't think I'm familiar with Turnip. What size town is that, ma'am?"

Mother bristled, calculated, and replied with pursed lips, "Thousand," not looking at the salesman. I jerked my head up toward Mother, and she gave me a look that said, "Don't you dare say one word!" I couldn't believe she had said a thousand, knowing perfectly well the population was exactly 381. Furthermore, Mother was a cornerstone in the Turnip Church of Christ, and she and I both knew lying would earn you a ticket straight to hell. I kept quiet.

We finished our shopping, buying a brown suit with "growing room," complete with loose lace-up shoes, soft socks, a white shirt with stiff collar, a brown belt, and a striped tie. The only thing I didn't leave with was a pine box and six friends.

As we exited and stepped onto the sidewalk, I asked in disbelief, "Mother, why did you tell that

man Turnip was a thousand when you know it's
381?"

   She stopped me in my tracks, looked me dead in
the eye, and said in a stern voice, "Cody, when you
get older, you'll learn that if city folks find out you're
from a *small* town, they'll take advantage of you."

My Best Day

*"Was it the Monday I had waited so long for
or just another cruel dream?"*

It was about to be the biggest day of my life, and I couldn't sleep. Clicking my flashlight on and off, I watched the hands on my nightstand clock labor their way toward dawn. It was 2:30 A.M. My brother Jim, sleeping in the twin bed next to me, hadn't swished his covers since 10:00 P.M. Mother and Daddy were at the other end of the frame house, but I could easily hear Daddy's snore.

My window was open, and the night air had cooled enough that I no longer stuck to the sheets. The attic fan lumbered in the background, pulling a gentle breeze through my window. Only one car had rumbled down the street since I had gone to bed. June bugs were bumping into my window screen as if there were candy inside. As I craned my neck toward where the sun would rise I could see lightning bugs playing in the summer night.

189

The air smelled as if rain might be near. I hoped not. Three-thirty came and sometime after that, sleep.

I awoke with a start and did an instant inventory. Did I fall asleep? Yes. Was the sun coming up? Yes. Was it the Monday I had waited so long for or just another cruel dream? Yes, it was the day. I grabbed the torturing clock and strained to clear my vision. Ten past six. "Yes!" I uncontrollably blurted out, trying to extinguish enough enthusiasm so as not to wake Jim. Daylight was coming, and so was my sky blue motor scooter.

My mind raced. Should I get up? No one was up. Could I stay in bed? Doubtful. How long could I lie here without peeing on myself? All good questions, but not the big one: When would Sears Roebuck and Company deliver my dream? When?

I had heard Mother on the phone with the man at Sears last Saturday and, as she had told me fifty times since, "He said they were assembling the scooter, and they would deliver it on Monday." I pondered Monday. The twenty-four-hour day was already almost seven hours old. Only an adult would be so insensitive as to say just "Monday," and only another adult would allow such a timetable.

Sears opened at 8:00 A.M. six days a week. I had memorized the white letters on the glass door of Sears in Evansville. I calculated thirty miles at fifty-five miles an hour equaled thirty minutes. Ten minutes to load. Ten minutes to find my house in Turnip, where there were few street names and no house numbers. Now I worried. How would a foreigner delivering a scooter actually find me? He

would have to ask a local. No problem. Everyone in
Turnip knows where everyone lives.

Back to time. An hour. It should take no more
than an hour for the delivery truck to get here. But
when would they leave? Questions with no answers.
Frustrating. I'd assume the best. They could be here
at 9:00. I couldn't wait.

I shot out of bed and straight to the bathroom. I
pushed my erect spout down and aimed at the water.
Erections and urination don't work well together. I
waited. Then it blasted out, hitting the floor, then
the rim, and then the water. Mother wouldn't be
happy, but that would be another day.

The flush was loud. As I made my way toward
my toothbrush, Jim looked at me, then at his clock,
then back at me, and said, "What are you doing, stupid?" Big brothers have a way with words. He didn't
require an answer, and I rushed through my morning
routine which on a school or church day could take
forty-five minutes, but today took about forty-five
seconds. I needed to be on the lookout in case the
Sears man got lost.

The back screen door creaked as I pushed my
tired old dog Blackie out of the way. He didn't move
from where the screen door relocated him. He only
tilted his head toward me with the same look as my
brother.

I hopped down the concrete steps and onto the
sidewalk, moving quickly toward our one-car garage.
My eyes were scanning rapidly. I could see two
streets. No Sears man. I ran to the front yard, where
the signless streets met. There wasn't a car or truck
in sight, just old man Wilkes limping toward the

courthouse square. I listened. Birds. Nothing but birds. I listened harder. A dog in the distance. A rooster. No truck. Then I realized the chances of the scooter arriving at 7:00 A.M. were zero. Where to wait? I decided on the front porch facing east. The sun was beginning to rise over the Wooleys' house across the street. The day was heating up quickly. I thought of Blackie on the back porch in the shade. He was looking smarter. None of the leaves on our giant pecan trees were moving. Time was crawling.

I had no watch. Only one person in my grade did. It made no sense to me for a boy to have a watch when I had the sun and the town fire siren at noon. But for the first time I wished for one. I calculated. It must be close to 7:30. I could hear Daddy's heavy feet creaking across the floor as I walked past the open living room windows. He would be gone by 7:45. I decided to embrace the fact that the truck wouldn't arrive this early even if I was lucky. I went back to sit with Blackie where the concrete was cool and the shade was total.

I had dreamed of this day for over two years— ever since Jerry Formby let me ride his Sears moped around the yard. I couldn't believe the thrill of effortlessly turning the handle grip and increasing the speed and noise of the moped. It was like having another set of big, strong legs that never got tired. I rode the moped that day until Jerry got mad at not being able to make me stop. I was never the same after that day.

A terrible smell brought me back to reality. Blackie had passed gas. I looked at his face and saw no shame. I snorted to clear my nose and drifted

back to my two years of pleading to Mother and
Daddy with not one glimmer of hope. Between
pleadings I would escape to my book of dreams—the
Sears Roebuck catalogue. I had worn out the scooter
page, studying every line of every scooter, ultimately
settling on the Allstate "Cruisaire." It was beautiful
with its aerodynamic shape and bubble butt. It came
complete with speedometer, buddy seat, and spare
tire, and was a really pretty light blue to boot. The
catalogue boasted of 50 mph speed and 110 miles
per gallon. With gasoline costing 27¢ a gallon I figured I could go around the world and live as happily
as the Swiss Family Robinson.

A few cars moved slowly past my house as the
morning began to awaken, the sound of each one
stirring my excitement only to end in disappoint-
ment. No Sears man. Daddy had left for work with
a rub of my burr head and a parting, "Have a good
day, Cody." He knew what was coming, but he was
not a man to show emotion. I wondered why men
did that.

My waiting continued. I thought about my afternoon newspaper route. Every day I pedaled around
town and out the highways up and down hills. The
work wasn't so hard as it was relentless. The newspaper never took a vacation. But my pockets were
full of nickels and my strong box was full of folding
money. My legs were strong, my aim was accurate,
and my marketing was deft. I made $30 a month
with about a third of that going into my savings
box—a metal box complete with a brother-proof key.
I had almost $100 saved when I was ten. That's
when my pleadings began in earnest.

My first approach was Mother, the easy target. I quickly learned that she would have nothing to do with the scooter decision. It seemed everything that had wheels fell in Daddy's domain. Her answer for months was the same, "Cody, you'll have to ask your father." That struck fear in my heart. She was quick to add the redundant, "But I don't think he will let you have a scooter until you are much older."

Fearful, I began to think about my new target—Daddy. Daddy was not a happy man. And he was not free with money. He saved his money and paid cash or went without. He and Mother grew up with dirt floors, bootstrap college diplomas and, to hear them tell, had only bread and water to eat and dirt to play with. I didn't know much about the Depression, but the term certainly seemed to fit. They didn't want to spoil Jim and me. Any money we had to spend came from scavenging Coke bottles, mowing lawns, or delivering newspapers. We made our own money and could buy as many milkshakes, candy bars, and Cokes as we wanted, but a motor scooter was quite another deal.

My breakthrough with Daddy came when I was eleven. My first approach had been to show him the scooter in the catalogue and hope for mercy. None there. I then tried mentioning the scooter on a weekly basis. That was met with "the stare." Jim and I almost preferred the belt to the stare. Daddy hadn't gotten mad yet, but I was also no closer to the scooter. Then I tried, "Jerry Formby has one, so why can't I?" That blew up as well, and the stare was supplemented with a reddening face—but no words. I hated the no words part. Did this man have a heart? Then I plotted a scheme looking at the situation from Daddy's point of view, and I got lucky.

Saturdays were Daddy's best days. And the best time was before the afternoon baseball game on television. I had chosen my approach. Daddy was sitting in his chair, the one no one else could sit in. I had the catalogue, my strong box, and my calculations. I hoped the numbers would appeal to Daddy's degree in mathematics. I laid out the plan to him gently, careful to apply no pressure or seek sympathy while displaying just the right amount of fear. My fear was real. He was a powerful man both physically and emotionally.

I showed him the price of $309.50. Then I counted out my savings to him—$178.00. I showed him that by working and saving $20 a month I could pay for the scooter in less than a year. He didn't get mad. A good sign. He took the catalogue and studied the worn pages. I was quiet. I felt my heart beating faster. I was also breathing faster. I hoped he wouldn't notice. If he said no, it would be hard not to cry, but crying would work against me, too. Daddy wanted Jim and me to be men no matter what our age.

My timing must have been perfect. As he looked at the motor scooter, he said wistfully, "When I was young I wanted a Harley Davidson. I never had enough money to buy one, but I always dreamed of having one." I realized for the first time that he was like me. His eyes returned to the tattered page, then to me. I listened. "Cody, this is a lot of money and a lot of responsibility." I acknowledged with a nod. Words might betray me. My emotions were becoming extreme. I could feel every hair on my body. I kept full eye contact although it was difficult to look into his powerful presence. Then he said with some reservation, "I'll tell you what," at which point my spirit soared with hope and at which time my bodily fluids were in danger of exiting. "When you are twelve years old, and if you continue making all A's in school," he paused, "and if you pay $200, then I'll pay the rest." I could not believe what I had just heard. I wanted to ask him to repeat what he had said.

However, in a state of shock and disbelief I could only muster, "Yes, sir, I understand." My insides wanted to laugh and cry simultaneously. I pressed my lips to hold in my emotions and extended my hand. Looking Daddy straight in the eye I uttered, "Thanks, Daddy. I won't let you down." I wanted to hug him, but he was not the hugging type.

He handed me the catalogue and said, "I guess you had better go tell your mother what we decided."

Jim and Mother were in shock when I told them. Mother was happy but worried. Jim was surprised but not jealous for he had just gotten his beginner's driving permit. I floated as happily as a butterfly for days.

I then only worried about the wait. It would be the longest year of my life. The date was set—the first Monday of my twelfth summer. I wasn't worried about Daddy's changing his mind, for if nothing else he was a man of his word. He expected the same of Jim and me. The most repeated advice I remember him giving was, "If you aren't anything else, be hon-

est. In the end that's all there is of a man." I didn't
know about that, but I did know his position would
never change.

My flashback ended with Mother's voice calling
me to lunch. "Cody, come and eat! It's on the table."
I didn't care much about food, but Mother did. I
choked down my bologna and cheese sandwich,
gulped my glass of milk, and hit the back door running. About the time the door slammed, I heard
Mother's familiar, "Andrew Cody, don't slam that
door!" Too late.

I was on my bicycle, my mission being to circle
the courthouse square in search of the Sears man. No
luck. I returned after waiting at Turnip's only blinking light for what seemed like a day but was probably only an hour or so. I entered the back door
gently, in need of Mother's help.

"Mother, where's the Sears man?" I asked in a
painful tone. Emotions were okay with Mother as
long as Daddy wasn't around.

"I don't know, Cody," she said sympathetically.

"Can you call and see if they forgot?" I pleaded.
Long-distance calls were reserved for sickness and
dying, but Mother could see my pain. It was 2:15 in
the afternoon.

"Let's give them a call," she said cheerfully. She
picked up the phone and asked Mrs. Minerva for
"long distance" after exchanging pleasantries. She
waited. When the Sears man answered, Mother
began to speak fast. There were no pleasantries
when money was wasting. She asked all the right
questions with kindness and firmness and several
"Yes, sirs" and "I understands" then, "Goodbye." I

was focused and not breathing as she turned and said with a smile, "They left the store in Evansville half an hour ago and should be here any time." I hugged Mother, something we didn't do much of in our house, and ran out the back door, skidding and turning back just in time to catch the screen door before it slammed. I smiled a quick smile and Mother returned it.

I began circling the house. Mother had taken off her apron and joined the search. Jim was nowhere around, and Daddy was at work, which was good—I could be me.

On about my third revolution around the house I got a glimpse of a green pickup with wooden rails. I ran toward the truck and could see lettering on the door. No truck in Turnip had lettering on the door except the fire truck. This must be it! My bare feet were flying high above the ground as I glimpsed the baby blue scooter peeking through the horizontal boards. I began waving and shouting at the two men in the slow-moving truck. The driver smiled a knowing smile even before I shouted, "Hey, mister, this is it, this is it! That's my scooter." The driver turned the corner slowly with me running alongside the truck.

He came to a stop beside our garage. I hopped on the running board, my fingers gripping the wooden rails, and pressed my face to the planks for the first look at my scooter. It was magnificent! No more catalogues. No more begging. No more sleepless nights. This was the real thing and it was mine! I checked it over—baby blue, buddy seat, spare tire, speedometer, headlight, handbrake, and foot brake, shiny and smelling of fresh lubricants.

I hopped down and said, "Mister, that's *my* scooter!" and waited for his reply.

He pulled a clipboard out of the truck seat and said, "Are you Hank Walker?"

I quickly said, "No, sir, that's my daddy." I waited.

Suppressing a smile, the Sears man asked, "Is this scooter for Mr. Walker?"

A sense of humor was an endangered species in Daddy's house as I replied, "No, sir, I'm Cody Walker and that's my scooter." Mother and the man chuckled at me, and I was embarrassed at not catching the joke. Perhaps I was more like my father than I wanted to think.

The driver smiled at Mother and said, "Ma'am, it looks like this delivery is for you folks. Where would you like for me to unload?"

Mother replied, "Why don't you back in here and unload on the sidewalk?"

He backed the truck into place and lowered the tailgate. I had my first full view of the Allstate Cruisaire, and my only thought was "Perfect." As the two Sears men carefully placed the scooter on the ground, my eyes inventoried each part. It was a magical moment.

I was in a trance as the driver said, "Well, son, she's ready to go." With the scooter on the kickstand I eased onto the leather seat and gripped the soft handlebars, checking the clutch and brake levers. "She's full of gas and runs like a champ," he added.

I looked at him and asked meekly, "Can I start her up?"

With a big easy smile he said, "Sure thing. She's all yours."

Those were the words I had waited a lifetime to hear. I glanced at Mother and sensed her concern. "I'll be careful, Mom," I offered. I hopped to the right side of the scooter, pulled the choke, and kicked the starter. The engine revved, blowing blue smoke out the tailpipe. It sounded like heaven.

I rolled her off the kickstand and was putting her into first gear when Mother said firmly, "Andrew Cody, you be careful."

"Don't worry, Mom."

I eased out the clutch and felt the power of the engine as the wheels began to roll. The scooter lurched forward, then smoothed out, and at last I was moving—not under my power but the scooter's. Unbelievable. For an instant my mind relived that first ride on Jerry Formby's moped. The feeling was the same but better—this time I didn't have to get off. I eased into the street, looking both ways, and found second gear. I glanced back, causing the scooter to wobble. I could see all three adults with two waving and one covering her mouth. "Thanks, Mom," I yelled. I couldn't worry. I was in heaven.

I checked the speedometer: 20 mph. I checked the odometer: 1.3 miles. I tested the front and rear brakes. Perfect. I rounded my first corner and turned the handle grip for more speed. Wow! The feeling was absolute exhilaration. The wind was moving across my face and through my hair. I was free! I was no longer earthbound. Just like in my dreams, I felt like I was flying. My smile was permanent. I had never been so happy.

I rode and rode and rode that day. I circled by the

house many times, honking the horn and smiling at Mother's wave from the kitchen window.

When night came, I lay down next to Jim, still feeling the vibration of the scooter in my hands and arms. It had been the best day of my life. I was in heaven with wings — or at least wheels. My dream had come true.

Decades later, it's still my best day. 🐾

Just Peeking

"He rotated his head from the keyhole, raised his eyebrows, and opened his mouth as if he had just seen heaven."

Trouble always began innocently for me. And so it was on a hot, aimless summer day of my twelfth year. Lunch had passed, and it was naptime for most of the porch sitters in Turnip. Boredom drove my bicycle and me to the Dibbles' house. I was more at home at the Dibbles' than in my own house. I felt more accepted there and was accorded more respect than any eleven-year-old in town. And although Gary was sixteen and Gwen was fourteen (going on twenty), I was treated better than a little brother.

Gary was my mentor. He taught me model airplane building, and we spent hundreds of hours building and flying all sizes of hand gliders, tow line gliders, free flights, and control line airplanes that we made from kits or patterns. Gary and I took our work seriously but had fun in the process. Mr. Dibble was the principal of the Turnip school and a man of few words, telling us on more than one occasion, "Boys, a job worth doing is a job worth doing right." I listened.

Gwen was Gary's younger sister. She was a blue-eyed blonde with the breasts of my dreams. She was gifted and proud of the gift, as evidenced when older boys were at the Dibbles'. The only thing I had in common with Gwen was Gary. She hardly knew I existed. That was about to change.

The Dibbles' house was a hangout for kids who lived in town, most of whom were teachers' children. That was the case with me. Mother taught math. Mrs. Dibble was a nurse at the school.

Summers were playtime for town kids, unlike my friends who lived in the country and had eggs to gather, chickens to feed, cows to milk, horses to tend, or crops to gather. My dad tried to find more chores for me, but I made myself scarce when I saw that look in his eye. I could not, however, avoid lawn mowing, leaf raking, pecan gathering, or house painting. But I saw no logic in digging and planting strips of St. Augustine grass into dirt when dirt had better uses such as clod fights, war games, and basketball. The only thing grass did was grow. And it required constant watering and mowing with the accompanying admonition, "You boys stay off that grass! You'll kill it!" Adults thought differently.

As I drove my bike to the Dibbles' side porch and flipped the kickstand down, I noticed things were unusually quiet. I opened the unlatched screen door, as I had a thousand times before, and saw Gary's empty bed which had recently been moved to the porch for cooler sleeping. Gary was not in his room, and I noticed his bike was gone. I continued through the house toward the kitchen, where Mrs. Dibble usually kept homemade cookies for the chosen (I was definitely one of those—her favorite, I might add). No cookies and no Mrs. Dibble. Mr. Dibble was eternally principaling the school, so it was no surprise he wasn't there.

I walked further through the small frame house with creaky wooden floors, lots of open double-hung windows, and well-worn but friendly furniture. Gary's radio was off, as was the family TV. I guessed I had struck out in my fight against boredom.

Then I noticed the bathroom door was closed. I paused. I heard water splashing. I quickly deduced: the station wagon was not in the driveway, so Mrs. Dibble was gone; Gary's bike was gone, so he must be gone, too; and Mr. Dibble was certainly not taking a bath at 2:00 in the afternoon. My heart began to race. For the first time in my eleven-year-old life, I was alone in a house with a beautiful naked girl.

I could hardly contain myself. My chest and head felt strange. My breathing changed. My senses were on highest alert. I had never actually seen a real titty—especially a big, young, proud titty. My mind raced. Sure I had seen Ben's hidden stash of *Playboy* magazines, but they weren't the real thing. This was—and no one was around, and no one would know.

I was motionless and no more than five paces from the bathroom door and heaven. I turned only my head and studied the door. Completely closed. I wouldn't be detected. I had an escape route to the back door if Mrs. Dibble came in the front and an escape to the front if Gary came in the back. This was encouraging, and I didn't need encouragement.

My eyes focused on the door latch. Thank God it was an old-fashioned skeleton key lock like my grandmother's, and there was no key in the hole. I felt like rapture was occurring. Rapture. Preacher. The devil. Hell, I could feel the devil at my side. Or was it guilt? I couldn't distinguish. I was approaching sin. This is what the red-faced preacher had railed about. What to do? I had never seen a titty. God created titties. And he certainly blessed Gwen. I just wanted a peek. What could be the harm? Would God strike me blind? If I made it to the keyhole, I would only look through with one eye, and losing one eye was definitely worth the risk. I shouldn't—but I could not resist.

Gwen was splashing about. I was spellbound. My heart raced. I was breathing so fast my eyes began to blur. I must slow my breathing, I thought, because I couldn't go blurry at the most important moment of my young life.

I approached the door like Marcel Marceau. Not a creak. No sound except water and my heart, which was about to leap out of my body. I thought of Mother and Mrs. Dibble and my eternal soul. I had never made a decision of this magnitude. But the Sunday morning invitation song didn't hold a candle to this moment. I pressed forward.

I lowered my body in controlled jerks until my pupil was centered on the keyhole. With the intensity of Galileo I searched the room for the masterpieces, but saw none. The tub was in sight, but I couldn't see Gwen. She was humming and singing

Buddy Holly's *"That'll Be the Day"* and splashing happily. I strained. Nothing. My ears were perked for intruders. Nothing. Then I heard her skin rub against the tub as she slid down to the bottom. I was desperate for a glimpse. In my straining, with my eye overriding my brain, I bumped my head ever so gently into the doorknob. All water motion stopped. I cringed and froze.

Gwen asked in an unknowing tone, "Is someone there?"

Thank God she didn't know. I was quieter than a deceased mouse. Fear of capture overcame me. I didn't move for almost a lifetime. Soon the water was churning, and the humming resumed. After several minutes I slithered ever so quietly away from heaven and hell. My mouth was dry. My skin was wet and pale. My limbs were trembling. Soon I was out the door, undetected. I thought about how stupid it was to risk my mortal self and immortal soul but how heavenly it would have been to see a beautiful titty. I felt like Moses on the mountaintop not being allowed to enter the Promised Land.

At that moment the devil presented himself to me in the person of Carl Clinton. He had walked up just as I was tiptoeing off the porch, and he said in a full voice, "What's going on?"

Startled but trying in my best voice I said, "Hi, Carl. Oh, nothing much." He wasn't buying it.

"Why you tiptoeing off the porch?" I was without excuse. The pause betrayed me. I wasn't good at lying.

"Oh, come on and tell me. What's in the house? What have you been doing?"

Carl was fifteen, one year older than Gwen and four years older than me. He was also the boy who topped all mothers' lists of kids not to hang out with. I was quite certain that either the devil had sent him or he was in fact the devil. As I confessed my story in bits and pieces, Carl quickly grasped the situation.

"Come on," he said in a forceful whisper, "I wanna see."

"Carl, I said I didn't *see* her titties."

"Sure," he interrupted mockingly. "Come on, let's go. You're in this deal too deep to get out now."

He knew he needed me to get into the Dibbles' house because the Dibbles trusted me, and I certainly knew my way around. He was moving toward the screen door, motioning for me to accompany him. As I edged toward the back door it felt like I was betraying my second family. But I really wanted to see a titty, and this might be my only chance.

We were soon at the bathroom door, and water was splashing. My excitement returned with a heightened sense of fear. Carl was beyond my control. He hogged the keyhole. I nudged him and mouthed, "Let me see." His eye returned to the keyhole. I nudged harder. He rotated his head from the keyhole, raised his eyebrows, and opened his mouth as if he had just seen heaven. My face said, "Let me see." He smiled and motioned me to the keyhole. My eyelid batted for clarity and then, oh my God, there they were—in the flesh. Beauty. Absolute beauty. Damp from hair dripping water. I had never seen anything so perfect. They were larger than I expected, and the nipple was better than any

Playmate's. They reminded me of scoops of ice cream with cherries on top. I guessed the reason they stuck out was the milk. The bigger they are, the more milk they carry. Then Gwen cupped water and rinsed her neck and breasts. All my senses were outside my skin. I loved God for his creation.

Then Carl jostled me and giggled. I froze. His eyes connected with mine when we both heard water pouring off Gwen's body as she stood to get out of the tub. We froze. I heard the towel being jerked from the towel bar as she asked in a frightened and angry tone, "Who's there?"

We said nothing.

"Gary? Mother? Are you there?" she said hopefully.

Not a word.

She asked louder, "Who's there?" Carl giggled again. I could have killed him. He didn't really care if we got caught. He'd been caught at everything. I was the saint whose crown was melting.

Carl implored in a whisper with an immediacy, "Get me a pencil and some paper."

"Why?" I asked incredulously.

"Just do it," he

said in a big brother tone. I did. Then he instructed, "I want you to write her a note and tell her we're sorry we scared her and we didn't see anything." I thought this was the second dumbest idea I ever heard.

"No," I said, "I'm not gonna do that." Carl immediately got serious.

"You write that note, or I'll tell them this was all your idea and that you were here before me and invited me in. You know Mr. Dibble will kick you out of school, and your daddy will beat the life out of you." His logic at that moment was convincing. He added, "Besides, she ain't gonna know who's out here." It made sense, kinda.

I picked up the pencil as Gwen asked again, "Who's out there?"

Carl whispered to me, "Hurry," in a harsh and older tone. I finished the note. Carl proofed it, folded it, and passed the evidence incriminating me under the door. I reached to grab it. Too late, Gwen pulled it inside. Then, after a few seconds, she began yelling, "You get out of my house! My daddy's gonna kill you! My mother is gonna be home any minute, and she will kill you, too!"

I felt sick. The situation was out of control. I didn't *feel* like I was doing something wrong—I *knew* I was. I felt sorry for Gwen. I felt bad for myself. And I was beginning to understand Mother's feelings about Carl.

Then I heard a car door shut. It was the all-too-familiar closing of the white '56 Chevy door, followed by the sound of crinkling grocery sacks. I looked at Carl and he looked at me. We bolted from the bathroom door and out the back screen door, which announced our exit with a bang.

I heard Gwen yelling in the distance as I jumped on my bike and began pedaling as fast as I could. Even so, Carl was outdistancing me on foot. He turned right toward his house and I took a left turn toward town. As I rounded the corner, I looked back to see Mrs. Dibble holding two bags of groceries. "What are you boys doing?" she yelled in an angry voice. Then the fatal, "Cody Walker, you come back here!"

I didn't stop. I didn't look back. I pretended not to hear. She could be mistaken. Then I remembered my handwriting. I pedaled harder. I knew my reputation, if not my life, was over. Heaven was out of the question. Doom engulfed me.

I bicycled to my secret hiding place, the abandoned unpainted house where Old Lady Buell once lived. It no longer felt so secret. I stashed my bike and pried open the back door. Entering the three-windowed empty room, I found my corner hideaway where I could see but not be seen. I sat on the linoleum floor, breathing hard. My place of refuge now felt like a jail cell.

My mind whirled for ways to escape today's events. Dead ends. All dead ends. I wished I had never been born. I lay on my side, curled up, and closed my eyes. For the first time death didn't seem like an enemy. I fell asleep.

My body jerked me awake. Had I dreamed the titty affair? No. Realizing the magnitude of the problem, I batted my eyelids and asked again, "Surely I had dreamed the titty affair?" My church conscience piously rebuffed, "Definitely not." I fearfully thought of my dad and realized my only option was to fess up.

As I rolled my bike into the backyard I saw Mother standing outside the kitchen door, fists on hips, with an omnipotent and furious look on her face. "Andrew Cody, what have you done?" she said, evoking guilt and requiring no answer. I laid down my bicycle and walked past her flaring nostrils as she held the back screen door open. I took my seat at the kitchen table. She lectured and I listened. The less I said, the better. It was our worst conversation. The only highlight was her decision not to tell Daddy because she knew he would beat the devil out of me with his forty-four-inch belt. I was thankful for that measure of mercy.

Over the next twenty-four hours I had to face Mother, Carl, Mrs. Dibble, and Gwen. My guilt was so real I could almost taste it. Unfortunately, I didn't die. I endured multiple punishments, the worst of which was being banned from the Dibbles' house for three months.

But at long last the punishment phase ended, my guilt lessened, and life returned to normal. On my return to the Dibble home three months later, Gary told me I was stupid, Mrs. Dibble warned me about my future behavior, but Gwen—Gwen gave me a becoming smile and an enticing wink. Only then did I begin to feel okay about myself. When Gwen and I were out of earshot of everyone else, she asked, "Was the peek worth the trouble?"

I visualized ice cream and cherries and replied, "What trouble?"

We both smiled. 🦋

Sugar

*"I enjoyed the nickname when no one was around.
But 'Sugar' for a nine-year-old boy?"*

My two favorite paper route customers were
Mrs. Erickson and Mrs. Hughes, eighty-one and
ninety-one years old, respectively. They were on my
bicycle route, which meant I was usually pedaling
fast and throwing hard so I could get home and play
with my friends. These two white-haired ladies
greeted me each day from their porches, some two
blocks apart, always cheerful and smiling. I came to
be one of the main social events of their day.

The paper cost $1.70 per month and there were
no tips, no matter how good the service, except from
these two ladies, who tipped me from 5¢ to 30¢
each month. What I shared with those two elderly
women, however, had little to do with news or
money.

Having thrown about half of my papers, I pedaled to Mrs. Hughes' house at my normal time.
There she was perched on her front porch in white

bedclothes and white bathrobe that matched her hair, looking frail with years. As usual, she was sitting in her wicker rocker on the porch, visiting with her neighbor and her daughter, who were not spring chickens themselves. I hopped off my bike, stood it on the kickstand, and walked toward the three smiling faces. I never threw her paper when she was on the porch for fear the paper would take a bad bounce and hit her. So today, like all other porch-worthy days, I unwrapped the sharp wire that bundled the paper and gently handed the news to Mrs. Hughes with an honest smile and a compassionate, "How are ya'll doing?"

"Fine. Just fine," came the chorused reply.

"How are you doing, Sugar?" asked Mrs. Hughes with a big, wrinkled smile filling her face.

Embarrassed, I replied, "I'm doing real well, Mrs. Hughes. Thank you."

Mrs. Hughes always called me "Sugar." She thought I was sweet. I enjoyed the nickname when no one was around. But "Sugar" for a nine-year-old boy?

I had never thought much about old people until my paper route introduced me to Mrs. Hughes and Mrs. Erickson and a few others. But I came to cherish my older customers and those two in particular. And they knew it. Behind their sallow exteriors lived the compassion, kindness, and beauty of princesses. I grew to love them, and they, me.

Six years later, when I was fifteen and Mrs. Hughes was no longer able to sit on the front porch, I walked up the old wooden steps to the frame house where I had carried so many papers and knocked on the wooden screen door. I entered Mrs. Hughes' bedroom at the invitation of her daughter. Several people were in the room keeping the ninety-seven-year-old company. Mrs. Hughes asked who I was. Her eyesight and hearing were gone. I reached out and held her frail hand as I often did, then looked around the room and said, "It's Cody Walker."

"Who?"

I bent closer, knowing it wouldn't work. "It's Cody Walker," in a tone loud enough for her to hear clearly. She didn't know the name, as I could see in her cloudy blue eyes. So I swallowed my embarrassment, bent even closer, and said, "It's Sugar."

She beamed and squeezed my hand as tears rolled down her pale, wrinkled cheeks and said, "Ooooh, Sugar!"

She remembered my kindnesses. And I remember her. She is with me still. 🦋

Baseball

"I'll never forget the smell. Hot dogs, popcorn, smoke,
fresh-cut green grass. I raised my glove to my face
and breathed baseball."

Baseball was my father's religion. The ballpark
was the church, and the Yankees were gods. The
year was 1961.

The summers of my boyhood revolved around
baseball except for the one-week church revival in
June when Mother wanted her two young Christians
beside her, and Daddy needed his center fielder and
short stop. That was my only tense week of summer,
with Mother winning and Daddy kicking dirt.

Daddy went to college on a baseball scholarship
and dreamed of my brother Jim and me becoming
professional baseball players. Daddy founded baseball in Turnip. The three of us built the fields,
mowed the grass, raked the dirt, and chalked the
lines. We studied the rulebook, learned every position, and were taught that winning was everything.
Daddy's motto was, "If we can't beat 'em, we're

gonna whip 'em." And, "Get in front of that ball and let it hit you in the nose. Get some blood on you, then you'll know how to play." Needless to say, he had more passion for the game than Jim and I, but we loved the game because he loved it.

It was June when our family of four piled into the Chevy and struck out on an unforgettable trip to glory. We were headed to Kansas City, where the Yankees were playing four games in three days against the Kansas City Athletics.

Daylight was just over the horizon as Daddy started the car and Mother loaded the ice chest and Thermos for our twelve-hour drive to Kansas City. Jim and I were in the back seat with caps on our heads, fists in our gloves, and hearts in the clouds. Jim was fifteen and I was twelve. We pulled out of the drive in darkness, with Mother reading the map by flashlight and Daddy working the gears and burning Lucky Strikes.

The two-lane road went through the center of a hundred little towns in Texas, Oklahoma, and Kansas. Most had stoplights and city cafés, but we had our ice chest stuffed with bologna and cheese sandwiches and enough fixin's to last for two days. We only stopped to fill up with gasoline and drain our bladders, the gas tank setting the schedule.

Hot summer air filled the car as we drove with the windows down, radio off, and little conversation. Kansas City was a longer trip than we had ever made. I wondered what the state line looked like and if people from out of state looked different—like foreigners.

We crossed into Oklahoma before lunch. I was

surprised there wasn't a chalk line. The trees didn't change. The grass didn't change. The people and cars didn't change, but the road did get bumpier, as my Texas Highway Department Dad broke his silence to point out.

As we drove, my taciturn father seemed almost happy as he lit one Lucky from the end of the other. I hung my burr head out the back window, happy to be seated behind my smokeless Mother as I watched fences, pastures, and telephone poles blow by. I couldn't believe that tonight we would actually see the Yankees. I wondered if they were as big as they seemed on TV. How fast could they run? How far could they throw? I wondered what a real ballfield looked like.

It was almost 6:00 P.M. when we saw the city limit sign of Kansas City. Jim and I scooted forward, leaning on the front seat, taking in the sights of the big city and looking for the ballfield. In every town we had played ball we could see the light posts as we drove in. But Kansas City was huge and almost scary as we approached downtown. Cars and people were everywhere with red lights and signs on every cor-

ner. Daddy tensed, which meant everyone tensed. As we neared downtown, there was no talking because Daddy needed to concentrate. Jim and I swallowed our enthusiasm. We must have looked like a car full of owls as the two lanes became four, with cars on each side close enough to reach out and touch. We waved at people like we did in Turnip but with no response except the occasional stare or a nervous nod from the foreigners.

As we inched our way toward the stadium, my thoughts turned to baseball. Then Jim excitedly pointed ahead, "There it is! There's the lights!" We all leaned forward, and my dream began to come to life. But we had to drive in stop-and-go traffic for what seemed an eternity, finally creeping up to the stadium. We expected to see parking, but there was none. The ballfield lights towered above the enormously tall green walls of the stadium. We could not see in. The 7:00 game had started, and we were buried in traffic. Then we heard a roar from the crowd, the likes of which we had never heard. If we had fifty spectators on the homemade bleachers in Turnip, it was a big game. I knew that on the other side of the giant wall were Mickey Mantle, Roger Maris, Yogi Berra, Whitey Ford, Moose Skowron, Bobby Richardson, Tony Kubek, Clete Boyer, Elston Howard, Ralph Terry, Ryne Duren, and more. I wanted to jump out of the car and run to the field.

Finally, we parked about a mile from the stadium. Daddy wondered if we could find the car after the game. He removed the key and locked the car for the first time ever. Jim and I, ball gloves in hand, began running toward the lights, with Mother instructing us not to go far. Jim and I would run a hundred yards forward and fifty yards back to encourage Mother and Daddy to hurry. My heart beat faster as the lights grew nearer and the buzz of the crowd grew louder. At the ticket window Daddy purchased four box seats down the third base line. As we walked in, it felt like we were passing through the pearly gates.

We walked under the grandstands. At the end of the tunnel-like passage was a white light, the likes of which I had never seen. As we neared the opening, I clutched my glove to my chest and swallowed hard. Silently we entered heaven and saw a vision that was the most powerful of my young life. A thousand lights made the place brighter than day. The grass was so green it didn't look real, and it was mowed in perfect strips. The dirt was so red, and the white chalk lines were so straight, the infield so smooth, the elevated mound so perfectly shaped. The scoreboard was gigantic. The wire fences behind home plate almost reached the sky. I couldn't take it all in.

The crowd buzzed as a fastball popped into Yogi's mitt. Then my eyes turned to centerfield, and there he was. Unbelievable. Glove on one knee, hand on the other, waiting to run down a fly ball in the same stance Daddy had taught Jim and me. He kicked the grass between pitches, stretched, and moved like a tiger awaiting his prey. His cap socked down on his head just like on television. Mickey. I was transfixed.

And over in right field, in sleeves shorter than Mickey's, was Roger. Then there was No. 8, crouched behind the plate, moving just like on TV. The bat cracked and jolted my trance as a high fly went toward Roger. He drifted under the ball, gracefully catching it with two hands to retire the side. I stood frozen as the Yankees trotted toward the dugout—just the way I had imagined it, except a whole lot better. I finally breathed and scanned the crowd. There were more people in the stands than I had seen in my whole life. The weather was warm and perfect.

"Hot dog! Hot dog! Get your hot dog here!" a barker called, breaking my trance.

"Beer, ice cold beer here!" said another. I was shocked that they could sell beer. In Turnip it was not only illegal, it was a sin.

"Souvenirs, get your souvenirs! Souvenirs! Souvenirs!" The grandstands were alive with chatter.

And the smell . . . I'll never forget the smell. Hot dogs, popcorn, smoke, fresh-cut green grass, Cokes, candies, perfume, chalk, dirt, sweat, and leather— the leather glove, the leather shoes, and the leather ball all rolled into one. I raised my glove to my face and breathed baseball. I was so overcome that I couldn't believe I was still alive. But the players were alive and real. I could even see the hair on their arms, and what arms they had! Mickey's arms looked like Popeye's.

Daddy called for what must have been the third time. "Cody, come on! Our seats are down here." I could hardly take my eyes off the field as I walked in a trance down the steps, wearing my rubber cleats, and made my way to a fold-down wooden seat with a number on the arm. The seats were perfect—ten rows up, directly behind third base, and with a perfect view of the Yankee dugout.

Richardson was leading off the inning. I knew who was coming. Bobby rubbed the bat with rosin then knocked the dirt off his cleats. His shoes looked brand new as he stepped in the box and began to dig in. The umpire announced, "Play ball!" Bobby pushed the batting helmet down on his head. The pitcher fired and the ball popped into the catcher's mitt without a swing. "Stee-rike!" the ump shouted, as he shot his right hand into the air.

"Come on, Bobby, hit the ball! Hit the ball!" a fan shouted in an accent very different from that of East Texas. The next pitch was coming, then the bat cracked, and the crowd in unison roared, *"Wooooh,"* as Bobby hit a sharp single into the hole between third and short.

Next came Kubek, who flew out to left. Then came No. 9. Powerful, determined. Built more like a football player then a baseball player. He dug in the right side of the plate like an old bull, and the crowd grew loud with both cheers and jeers. I glared in disbelief at the fans who wished Maris ill. First pitch, and he launched it to right field. The crowd stood to watch. The ball was hit so high and so far that I couldn't believe it. The right fielder didn't even go to the wall. He knew it was a goner from the time it left Roger's bat. So did Roger, as he gentlemanly laid down his bat and broke into his home run trot. I stood on my seat and watched. I couldn't believe the first ball and the first time at bat he had hit a homer!

Mickey greeted Roger at home plate, as he had done so many times before. The buzz of the crowd only settled momentarily as No. 7 stepped to the plate. Huge arms. Huge legs. Huge neck. And huge bat. Power. Raw power and the ability to run like a deer. He was batting lefty against a right-hander. I watched his every move. He was beautiful. More beautiful than poetry or music. I could hardly breathe. He was my idol.

As he swung and missed for the third time, the ump announced with fervor, "Strike three!" It was a number Mickey had heard many times before. He carried his club on his shoulder like a caveman to the dugout with his head down, and I thought of Dizzy Dean's pronouncement: "Mickey Mantle looks better striking out than most people do hitting a home run."

The game went on, inning after inning, as I remained entranced. Daddy bought us hot dogs and Cokes. Best hot dog I ever tasted. My senses were heightened as never before and never since—my mind so clear, my vision so crisp. The sound of the bat hitting the ball and the ball slapping the glove. The crescendos of the crowd echoing the ebb and flow of life on the field. The taste of mustard and the smell—the smell of baseball.

I spent three glorious days in 1961 watching the greatest team play the greatest game in the world. I watched batting practice, where Mickey and Roger parked ball after ball after ball. I watched warm-ups and pitching practice. I saw Ryne Duren throw heat like I had never seen, Moose manning first base so powerfully, Yogi firing the ball to second, Mantle running down fly balls, Roger throwing strikes to home plate without a hop from right field. I bought a Yankee banner that hangs in my room today, alongside the glove I took to the stadium. I bought a packet of pictures of the Yankees and got Bobby Richardson and Roger Maris to sign theirs. I saw Maris sign autographs until there were no more to be signed. I saw Mickey sign one ball for a boy. The fans swarmed around him at every opportunity. I got close enough to Roger Maris to feel him breathe. He was big and strong. He had a flat top and wore a tight knit shirt. He seemed kind and had an easy smile for his fans. Jim got Moose Skowron to sign a ball. The next summer, when we ran out of balls, Jim and I used that ball until the signature rubbed off.

In Kansas City I saw fireworks fill the sky. I had never seen anything like it; a Roman candle was a big deal in Turnip. My senses never recovered from that weekend in 1961. Later in the year I watched Roger Maris on TV as he hit his sixty-first home run, breaking Babe Ruth's record. I was so happy for him and happy that, for a moment, I had known him.

Taking us to see the Yankees was the greatest thing my father ever did for me. Walking into the stadium and seeing the lights and the field and the players remains the most vivid moment of my life. I've never gotten over it.